Read with the Best

Teacher's Edition

American Literature I
1500 – 1860

Grades 8-12

Jill J. Dixon, B.S.Ed., M.Ed.

Copyright © 2012 by Jill J. Dixon and T.L. Dixon

ALL RIGHTS RESERVED. No part of this publication may be reproduced or transmitted in any form or by any means, electronic or mechanical, including photocopy, recording, or by any information storage and retrieval system, without prior permission in writing from the author and the publisher.

Permission is granted to the purchaser to reproduce only the Table of Contents/Weekly Schedule, Student Tests, and the Research Paper Checklist for immediate family student use, classes, and co-op classes. Permission is not granted to entire co-ops, schools, or school districts.

Printed in the U.S.A.

www.edudps.com

READ WITH THE BEST
- AMERICAN LITERATURE VOLUME I

INTRO

THE PURPOSE AND GOAL OF *READ WITH THE BEST*:

Read With The Best of American Literature is a two year high school literature, vocabulary, critical thinking and composition course designed to equip highschoolers with all the literary, thinking, vocabulary and writing skills needed for an adequate education. This course teaches extensive literary analysis and critical reading skills found on the new SAT, AP Literature exams, and in college level classes. In addition, it teaches SAT and ACT vocabulary words and expository writing, including the five paragraph essay required for college admittance.

Students who complete the two year American literature courses and the British literature course will be equipped to do the following:
- Take and pass the AP English Literature exam and receive college credit.
- Take and pass the AP English Language and Composition exam and receive college credit.
- Take and pass the CLEP American Literature exam for college credit.
- Take the SAT 25 minute timed essay with ease and confidence.
- Take the SAT Critical Reading and Vocabulary section with ease and confidence.

REQUIRED MATERIALS FOR *READ WITH THE BEST OF AMERICAN LITERATURE I*

1. *The Norton Anthology of American Literature, Volume 1* – **Shorter Seventh Edition only.** (Make sure you get the shorter 7th edition and Volume 1 only.)
   (Some parents may choose to find all of these works on line.)
2. *Write With the Best, Vol. 2* by Jill J. Dixon, B.S.Ed., M.Ed. This can be purchased at www.edudps.com (Will be used all 4 years of *Read With the Best Literature*)
3. *The New American Heritage Dictionary and Thesaurus.*
4. *Writing a Research Paper - A Step-By-Step Approach (3rd Edition) Grades 6-12* by Sadlier-Oxford Publishing (www.sadlier-oxford.com) (Will be used all 4 years of *Read With the Best Literature*)
5. *Writing a Research Paper Teacher's Edition* (3rd Edition) Grades 6-12 by Sadlier-Oxford Pub.
6. *The Scarlet Letter* (The Kaplan SAT Version) by Nathaniel Hawthorne (The Kaplan SAT Version has all SAT Vocabulary words and definitions outlined in the actual text.)

WHY IS THE STUDY OF LITERATURE SO IMPORTANT?

One major goal for our children is that their education will equip them to function in the twenty first century by being totally knowledgeable of their current surroundings and all that has come before to make our world and culture what it is now. The study of literature is the study of man, of human nature and of our world. An educated student is aware of all of these.

How to Use this Curriculum

This curriculum is divided into 34 weeks of critical reading. The 35th and 36th weeks (to make a total of 180 school days) are left open for testing and review, etc.
Students should attempt to complete all the course work in order to receive high school credit. It is suggested that high school students complete an American History course of the years 1500-1860 to accompany this literature course. It will make the reading material more meaningful and add depth and understanding.
I recommend *The History of US* by Joy Hakim – Volumes 2, 3, and 4. This is an excellent series with tests and workbooks that can be purchased separately. The series can also be purchased at www.audible.com and listened to as a family or by an individual student. In addition to this course, I also recommend *Don't Know Much About American History* by Kenneth Davis as an accompaniment.

Grammar and SAT Prep Suggestions

Some parents/teachers will see a need to add English grammar and additional SAT/ACT verbal preparation activities to this course.
The following are ones that I have used successfully with my high school students and highly recommend:
- *Easy Grammar Ultimate Series* (for high school) – Grades 9-12
- *Spark Notes SAT Prep.* in English and Writing
- *Fifty Five SAT Prep Activities: English* (from Pathways Publishing)
- *English Grammar Workbook for Dummies*
- *Peterson's The New SAT Writing Workbook* (This is a great book for practicing the 25 minute SAT required essay.)
- *SAT Verbal Question of the day* at www.collegeboard.com
- *Daily Warm-ups – SAT Prep Reading and Writing* by Walch Publishing
- *Editor-in-Chief* (Upper Levels)

Co-ops and Classes

Read With the Best of American Literature is ideal for co-ops and classes. It was actually written to be used in a homeschool class taught by the author. All activities except for Tests and the Culminating Activity at the end of each lesson can be completed by the student at home. Teachers can complete the Culminating Activity with their students when they meet once a week, and students can complete tests. They will also go over the answers to "Background Check", "Words to know", "Critical Reading", "Make It Real" and the "Writing Assignment" in class. Students can exchange writing papers and enhance proofreading skills. Classes and co-ops are ideal for literature discussion between students and the teacher. Classes are also a great place to practice the 25 minute SAT essay.

READ WITH THE BEST
– AMERICAN LITERATURE VOLUME I

WEEKLY WORK EXPLAINED

Students are required to complete work in five to six different areas each week. **All answers can be found in the Teacher's guide.**

- **Background Check**: Most weeks students are asked to answer questions about the author they are reading. Unless noted, the answers to all of these questions can be found in the Norton Anthology at the beginning section of each new author's work.

- **Words to Know**: Each week, students are assigned words from the reading to define. These words should be defined before the passages are read in order to enhance comprehension. Many of the words are common SAT words. Specific vocabulary words are tested approximately every four weeks. These tests with the specific words are found in the Teacher's Guide.

- **Literary Analysis**: Important literary terms that relate to the literary passages are given each week. These terms are tested approximately every six weeks. Tests and test keys are found in the Teacher's Guide.

- **Critical Reading**: Students are required to answer questions about each reading passage. These questions require critical thinking and critical analysis, and students improve these skills as the weeks progress.

- **Make It Real**: Each week, students are given an opportunity to apply learned skills or relate learned skills to what they already know.

- **Culminating Activity**: An activity is given at the end of each week to solidify all that the student has learned. These activities usually appeal to all learning styles to help students retain information.

- **Writing Assignments**: Students work on writing each week, but usually complete one writing assignment every two weeks. Writing assignments always relate to the literary passages and authors. Students work on a research paper for twelve weeks during the last half of the year, during weeks 21-32. Grading checklists for all writing assignments are found in the back of *Write With the Best, Volume 2*.

READ WITH THE BEST
– AMERICAN LITERATURE VOLUME I

STUDENT OBJECTIVES

Each student who completes this course will achieve the following objectives:

- Obtain 1 high school credit in literature, 1 high school credit in composition, and 1/4 credit in American history. (Additional credits can be obtained in American history by following the guidelines on the subsequent pages.)

- Learn to write a college level MLA style research paper on a literary topic.

- Master the five paragraph persuasive and expository essay as well as other expository writing such as note taking, writing outlines, summaries, literary critiques, book reviews, business letters, speeches, and newspaper articles.

- Master descriptive writing such as free verse poetry and dramatic monologues.

- Learn 173 SAT vocabulary words and understand 100's more.

- Master critical reading and thinking skills.

- Understand and analyze various genres of American literature such as short stories, autobiographies, historical accounts, rhyming and free verse poetry, novels, letters, and speeches.

- Understand and use 76 different literary terms necessary for literary analysis, interpretation, and optimal performance on the critical reading section of the SAT and AP Literature exams.

- Learn the backgrounds of and pertinent information regarding 27 authors of early American literature.

- Master editing and proofreading skills.

SPECIAL NEEDS STUDENTS

Students with special needs can use this curriculum successfully with specific adaptations such as:
- Reducing the reading requirements and amount of reading
- Referring to www.librivox.org for works read out loud
- Reducing some of the writing assignments
- Taking the tests orally

READ WITH THE BEST
— AMERICAN LITERATURE VOLUME I

INTRO

TEST SCHEDULE

Teachers are to administer the following tests on these specific weeks. Students are notified in their literature guide of these tests approximately two weeks before the test is administered.

Literary Terms Tests:

Test Covers:	Test Administered On:
Weeks 1-6	Week 8
Weeks 7-12	Week 13
Weeks 13-18	Week 20
Weeks 19-24	Week 26
Weeks 25-34	Week 35

Vocabulary Tests:

Test Covers:	Test Administered On:
Weeks 1-4	Week 6
Weeks 5-8	Week 10
Weeks 9-12	Week 14
Weeks 13-16	Week 18
Weeks 17-20	Week 22
Weeks 21-24	Week 27
Weeks 25-34	Week 35

Vocabulary tests are administered approximately every 6 weeks, and tests on literary terms are given approximately every 8 weeks. Tests and answer keys are found in the teacher's manual.

*Please note that not all vocabulary words from each week are covered on the vocabulary tests. Teachers may choose to give students the list of vocabulary words from each test to study.

Read With the Best   Diagnostic Prescriptive Services | www.edudps.com

MOST FREQUENTLY ASKED ?'S

- **What makes your highschool literature curriculum different from the others on the market?** *Read With the Best* is a thorough college-prep literature curriculum. I don't know of another high school curriculum marketed for homeschoolers that uses *The Norton Anthology*, a textbook that is used in most freshman college literature classes. I am also not aware of any curriculum that includes SAT vocabulary, activities that solidify learning for all learning styles, extensive literary analysis terms found on various tests, and a complete college-prep writing program as part of the literature program. *Read With the Best* also uses mainly whole works of literature (instead of excerpts) to ensure literary mastery.

- **How did you choose your literature for this program?** The literature in *Read With the Best of American Literature* was chosen for its literary, moral, analytic and didactic or inspirational quality. The works and authors that are included are also works and authors that any student who desires an adequate education should be familiar with. I chose works that teach students about various facets of life and encourage them to think critically and make moral decisions. Many of the readings in *Read With the Best of American Literature* inspire students and encourage them to take specific moral action. Most of these works were also picked from the AP English literature and CLEP American Literature guides.

- **Should only the college bound student take this course?** No. *Read With the Best of American Literature* is written for any highschool student who desires an adequate education. It teaches many skills such as vocabulary, critical reading, critical thinking, and writing – necessary life skills for any student.

- **Can my slow reader or poor writer complete this course?** Most definitely. Many of the works can be downloaded free on www.librivox.org so that students can listen to them auditorily. Several of them can also be purchased as books on audio CD. Slower readers are encouraged to listen to audio versions of the work as they read along. Writing assignments can be dictated by the student and typed or written by the teacher or fellow student. Writing assignments can also be reduced for those who truly struggle with getting their thoughts on paper.

- **Why is your American Literature course spread out over two years?** Highschoolers must have four years of literature to graduate, and these must include World Literature, British Literature and American Literature. In order for students to gain full understanding and appreciation for American Literature, it is crucial that it be divided into two years of study so that several important authors and works can be covered. American Literature is also a great tool for the introductory skills of critical and literary analysis.

Read With The Best – American Literature Volume I

Table of Contents & Weekly Schedule

Notes:
- **Background Check** - Students will find the answers to the background check in **The Norton Anthology** under author information at the beginning of each new author.
- **Literary Terms Tests** will be given on weeks 8, 14, 20, 26, & 35.
- **Vocabulary Terms Tests** will be given on weeks 6, 10, 18, 22, 27, & 35.

<u>Introduction</u> ....*i-vi*

<u>Week 1</u> **Christopher Columbus & John Smith**..1-9
*Christopher Columbus - Letter to Santangel & Letter to Ferdinand and Isabella
☐ Background Check
☐ Words To Know
☐ Literary Analysis
☐ Critical Reading Questions
*John Smith - From The General History
☐ Background Check
☐ Literary Analysis
☐ Words To Know
☐ Critical Reading Questions
☐ Make It Real
☐ Writing – **Descriptive Narrative**
☐ Culminating Activity

<u>Week 2</u> **John Smith & William Bradford**..…..........10-18
*John Smith - From "A Description of New England"
☐ Words To Know
☐ Literary Analysis
☐ Critical Reading Questions
*William Bradford - From Of Plymouth Plantation
☐ Background Check
☐ Words To Know
☐ Literary Analysis
☐ Critical Reading Questions
☐ Make It Real
☐ Writing - **Expository Essay**
☐ Culminating Activity

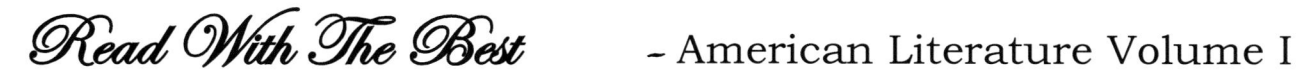

Read With The Best — American Literature Volume I

Table of Contents & Weekly Schedule

Week 3 **John Winthrop**......Skip..19-24
*John Winthrop - "A Model of Christian Charity"
- [ ] *Background Check*
- [ ] *Words To Know*
- [ ] *Literary Analysis*
- [ ] *Critical Reading Questions*
- [ ] *Make It Real*
- [ ] *Writing -* **Expository Essay**
- [ ] *Culminating Activity*

Week 4 **Anne Bradstreet**..25-32
*Anne Bradstreet - "The Prologue"
- [ ] *Background Check*
- [ ] *Literary Analysis*
- [ ] *Words To Know*
- [ ] *Critical Reading Questions*

*Anne Bradstreet - "Before the Birth of One of Her Children"
- [ ] *Words To Know*
- [ ] *Critical Reading Questions*

*Anne Bradstreet -   "Here Follows Some Verses Upon the Burning of Our House"
                    "To My Dear and Loving Husband"
- [ ] *Words To Know*
- [ ] *Critical Reading Questions*

*Anne Bradstreet - "The Author to Her Book", "To My Dear Children"
- [ ] *Words To Know*
- [ ] *Critical Reading Questions*
- [ ] *Make It Real*
- [ ] *Writing -* **Iambic Couplets / Iambic Pentameter**
- [ ] *Culminating Activity*
- [ ] **Study for a VOCABULARY TERMS TEST** *on Week 6 (covering Weeks 1-4)*

Week 5 **Mary Rowlandson**..33-39
*Mary Rowlandson - From "A Narrative of the Captivity and Restoration of Mrs. Mary Rowlandson"
- [ ] *Background Check*
- [ ] *Words To Know*
- [ ] *Literary Analysis*
- [ ] *Critical Reading Questions*
- [ ] *Make It Real*
- [ ] *Writing -* **Iambic Couplets**
- [ ] *Culminating Activity*
- [ ] **Study for a VOCABULARY TERMS TEST** *on Week 6 (covering Weeks 1-4)*

Read With The Best – American Literature Volume I
Table of Contents & Weekly Schedule

<u>Week 6</u> **Cotton Mather**......Skip..40-45
*Cotton Mather - The Wonders of the Invisible World
- [ ] Background Check
- [ ] Words To Know
- [ ] Literary Analysis
- [ ] Critical Reading Questions
- [ ] Make It Real
- [ ] Writing - **Elements of A Persuasive Essay**
- [ ] Culminating Activity
- [ ] **VOCABULARY TEST** over Weeks 1-4.
- [ ] **Study for a LITERARY TERMS TEST** on Week 8 (covering Weeks 1-6)

<u>Week 7</u> **Edward Taylor & Jonathan Edwards**..46-54
*Edward Taylor - "Huswifery." (together)
- [ ] Background Check
- [ ] Words To Know
- [ ] Literary Analysis
- [ ] Critical Reading Questions

✓ *Jonathan Edwards - "Sinners in the Hands of an Angry God."
- [ ] Background Check
- [ ] Words To Know
- [ ] Critical Reading Questions
- [ ] Make It Real
- [ ] Writing - **Outlines**
- [ ] Culminating Activity
- [ ] **Study for a LITERARY TERMS TEST** on Week 8 (covering Weeks 1-6)

<u>Week 8</u> **Benjamin Franklin**..55-61
*Benjamin Franklin - from The Autobiography of Benjamin Franklin (pgs 231 - 251 top)
- [ ] Background Check
- [ ] Words To Know
- [ ] Literary Analysis
- [ ] Critical Reading Questions
- [ ] Make It Real
- [ ] Writing - **Persuasive Essay**: Planning a thesis statement, outline, examples
- [ ] Culminating Activity
- [ ] **LITERARY TERMS TEST** - Weeks 1-6.
- [ ] **Study for VOCABULARY TERMS TEST** on Week 10 (covering Weeks 5-8)

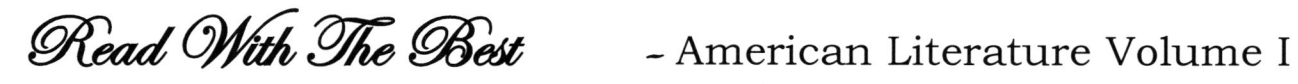

Read With The Best – American Literature Volume I
Table of Contents & Weekly Schedule

Week 9 **Benjamin Franklin**..62-67
*Benjamin Franklin - from The Autobiography of Benjamin Franklin (pgs 251 - top of 270)
- [ ] *Words To Know*
- [ ] *Literary Analysis*
- [ ] *Critical Reading Questions*
- [ ] *Make It Real*
- [ ] *Writing -* **Persuasive Essay**
- [ ] *Culminating Activity*
- [ ] **Study for VOCABULARY TERMS TEST** *on Week 10 (covering Weeks 5-8)*

Week 10 **Benjamin Franklin**...68-73
*Benjamin Franklin - from The Autobiography of Benjamin Franklin (pgs 270 - 292)
- [ ] *Literary Analysis*
- [ ] *Words To Know*
- [ ] *Critical Reading Questions*
- [ ] *Make It Real*
- [ ] *Writing -* **Book Review**
- [ ] *Culminating Activity*
- [ ] **VOCABULARY TERMS TEST** *over Weeks 5-8.*

Week 11 **John Adams & Abigail Adams.**..74-79
*John Adams & Abigail Adams - From "The Letters of John and Abigail Adams"
- [ ] *Background Check*
- [ ] *Literary Analysis*
- [ ] *Words To Know*
- [ ] *Critical Reading Questions*
- [ ] *Make It Real*
- [ ] *Writing -* **Book Review**
- [ ] *Culminating Activity*

Week 12 **Thomas Paine.** p324-338 80-86
*Thomas Paine - From Common Sense & "The Crisis, No. 1"
- [ ] *Background Check*
- [ ] *Words To Know*
- [ ] *Literary Analysis*
- [ ] *Critical Reading Questions*
- [ ] *Make It Real*
- [ ] *Writing -* **Persuasive Speech**
- [ ] *Culminating Activity*
- [ ] **Study for a LITERARY TERMS TEST** *on Week 14 (covering Weeks 7 - 12)*

Read With The Best — American Literature Volume I
Table of Contents & Weekly Schedule

<u>Week 13</u> **Patrick Henry & Thomas Jefferson**............(skip).................................87-95
*Patrick Henry - "Speech in the Virginia Convention"
(Find a printed copy online or listen to an audio version - www.librivox.org)
☐ Background Check
☐ Words To Know
☐ Literary Analysis
☐ Critical Reading Questions
*Thomas Jefferson - From The Autobiography of Thomas Jefferson & "The Declaration of Independence"
☐ Background Check
☐ Words To Know
☐ Critical Reading Questions
☐ Make It Real
☐ Writing - **Persuasive Speech**
☐ Culminating Activity
☐ **Study for a LITERARY TERMS TEST** on Week 14 (covering Weeks 7 - 12)

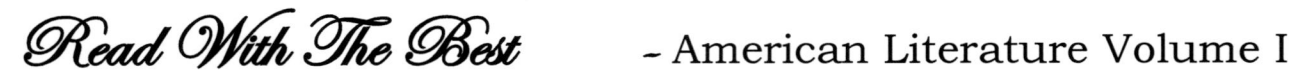

<u>Week 14</u> **Phillis Wheatly**...Completed.....................96-101
*Phillis Wheatly - "On Being Brought from Africa to America", "On the Death of Rev. Mr. George Whitefield, 1770" & "To His Excellency General Washington"
☐ Background Check
☐ Words To Know
☐ Literary Analysis
☐ Critical Reading Questions
☐ Make It Real
☐ Writing - **Persuasive Speech**
☐ Culminating Activity
☐ **LITERARY TERMS TEST** - Weeks 7-12.
   * NOTE: The reading selection is minimal this week due to holidays that usually fall during this time. If your schedule does not include a holiday, use this time to correct work, review, or catch up.

<u>Week 15</u> **Washington Irving**........Skip...102-108
✓ *Washington Irving - "Rip Van Winkle"
☐ Background Check
☐ Words To Know
☐ Literary Analysis
☐ Critical Reading Questions
☐ Make It Real
☐ Writing - **Literary Critique**
☐ Culminating Activity

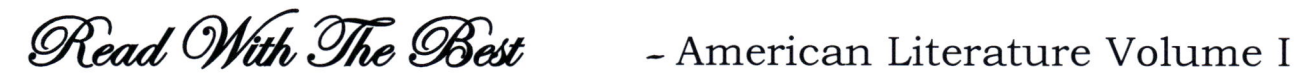

Read With The Best – American Literature Volume I
Table of Contents & Weekly Schedule

<u>Week 16</u> **James Fenimore Cooper & William Cullen Bryant**......Skip?......**109-117**
✓ *James Fenimore Cooper - From Last of the Mohicans
- ☐ *Background Check*
- ☐ *Words To Know*
- ☐ *Literary Analysis*
- ☐ *Critical Reading Questions*

*William Cullen Bryant - "Thanatopsis", "To A Waterfowl"
- ☐ *Background Check*
- ☐ *Words To Know*
- ☐ *Critical Reading Questions*
- ☐ *Make It Real*
- ☐ *Writing -* **Literary Critique**
- ☐ *Culminating Activity*
- ☐ **Study for a VOCABULARY TERMS TEST** on Week 18 (covering Weeks 9-16)

<u>Week 17</u> **Ralph Waldo Emerson & Henry Wadsworth Longfellow**...................**118-126**
*Ralph Waldo Emerson - "The American Scholar"
- ☐ *Background Check*
- ☐ *Words To Know*
- ☐ *Literary Analysis*
- ☐ *Critical Reading Questions*   p645   p646

*Henry Wadsworth Longfellow - "A Psalm of Life" & "A Slave's Dream"   p121-123
- ☐ *Background Check*
- ☐ *Words To Know*
- ☐ *Critical Reading Questions*
- ☐ *Make It Real*
- ☐ *Writing -* **Free Verse**
- ☐ *Culminating Activity*
- ☐ **Study for a VOCABULARY TERMS TEST** on Week 18 (covering Weeks 9-16)

<u>Week 18</u> **Nathaniel Hawthorne**...**127-134**
*Nathaniel Hawthorne - "Young Goodman Brown"
- ☐ *Background Check*
- ☐ *Words To Know*
- ☐ *Literary Analysis*
- ☐ *Critical Reading Questions*

✓ *Nathaniel Hawthorne - "The Minister's Black Veil"
- ☐ *Words To Know*
- ☐ *Critical Reading Questions*
- ☐ *Make It Real*
- ☐ *Writing -* **Free Verse**
- ☐ *Culminating Activity*
- ☐ **VOCABULARY TERMS TEST** - Weeks 9-16
- ☐ **Study for a LITERARY TERMS TEST** on Week 20 (covering Weeks 13-18)

Read With The Best – American Literature Volume I
Table of Contents & Weekly Schedule

Week 19 **Nathaniel Hawthorne**..**135-140**
*Nathaniel Hawthorne - The Scarlet Letter Chapters 1-4
- [ ] Words To Know
- [ ] Literary Analysis
- [ ] Critical Reading Questions
- [ ] Make It Real
- [ ] Writing - **Business Letter**
- [ ] Culminating Activity
- [ ] **Study for a LITERARY TERMS TEST** on Week 20 (covering Weeks 13-18)

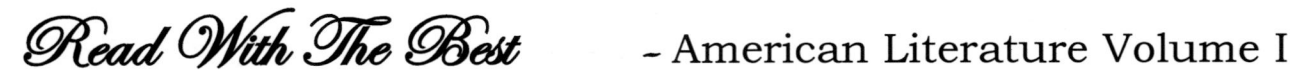

Week 20 **Nathaniel Hawthorne**..**141-147**
*Nathaniel Hawthorne - The Scarlet Letter Chapters 5-8
- [ ] Literary Analysis
- [ ] Words To Know
- [ ] Critical Reading Questions
- [ ] Make It Real
- [ ] Writing - **Business Letter**
- [ ] Culminating Activity
- [ ] **LITERARY TERMS TEST** -Weeks 13-18.
- [ ] **Study for a VOCABULARY TERMS TEST** on Week 22 (covering Weeks 17-20)

Week 21 **Nathaniel Hawthorne**..**148-153**
*Nathaniel Hawthorne - The Scarlet Letter Chapters 9-12
- [ ] Words To Know
- [ ] Literary Analysis
- [ ] Critical Reading Questions
- [ ] Make It Real
- [ ] Writing - **Research Paper / Schedule / Topics**
- [ ] Culminating Activity
- [ ] **Study for a VOCABULARY TERMS TEST** on Week 22 (covering Weeks 17-20)

Week 22 **Nathaniel Hawthorne**..**154-159**
*Nathaniel Hawthorne - The Scarlet Letter Chapters 13-16
- [ ] Words To Know
- [ ] Literary Analysis
- [ ] Critical Reading Questions
- [ ] Make It Real
- [ ] Writing - **Research Paper**
- [ ] Culminating Activity
- [ ] **VOCABULARY TERMS TEST**- Weeks 17-20

Read With The Best – American Literature Volume I
Table of Contents & Weekly Schedule

Week 23 **Nathaniel Hawthorne**..160-165
*Nathaniel Hawthorne - The Scarlet Letter Chapters 17-20
- [ ] Words To Know
- [ ] Literary Analysis
- [ ] Critical Reading Questions
- [ ] Make It Real
- [ ] Writing - **Research Paper**
- [ ] Culminating Activity

Week 24 **Nathaniel Hawthorne**..166-171
*Nathaniel Hawthorne - The Scarlet Letter Chapters 21-24
- [ ] Words To Know
- [ ] Literary Analysis
- [ ] Critical Reading Questions
- [ ] Make It Real
- [ ] Writing - **Research Paper**
- [ ] Culminating Activity
- [ ] **Study for a LITERARY TERMS TEST** on Week 26 (covering Weeks 19-24)

Week 25 **Edgar Allan Poe**....✓....SKIP?..172-179
*Edgar Allan Poe - "The Raven" and "Annabel Lee"
- [ ] Background Check
- [ ] Words To Know
- [ ] Literary Analysis
- [ ] Critical Reading Questions

*Edgar Allan Poe - "Ligeia"
- [ ] Words To Know
- [ ] Critical Reading Questions
- [ ] Make It Real
- [ ] Writing - **Research Paper**
- [ ] Culminating Activity
- [ ] **Study for a LITERARY TERMS TEST** on Week 26 (covering Weeks 19-24)
- [ ] **Study for a VOCABULARY TERMS TEST** on Week 27 (covering Weeks 21-24)

Read With The Best – American Literature Volume I
Table of Contents & Weekly Schedule

Week 26 **Edgar Allan Poe**............Skip..180-187
✓ *Edgar Allan Poe - "The Fall of the House of Usher"
- ☐ Literary Analysis
- ☐ Words To Know
- ☐ Critical Reading Questions

*Edgar Allan Poe - "The Purloined Letter"
- ☐ Words To Know
- ☐ Critical Reading Questions
- ☐ Make It Real
- ☐ Writing - **Research Paper**
- ☐ Culminating Activity
- ☐ **Study for a VOCABULARY TERMS TEST** on Week 27 (covering Weeks 21-24)
- ☐ **LITERARY TERMS TEST** - Weeks 19-24

Week 27 **Herman Melville**............Skip?...188-193
*Herman Melville - "Bartleby the Scrivener"
- ☐ Background Check
- ☐ Literary Analysis
- ☐ Words To Know
- ☐ Critical Reading Questions
- ☐ Make It Real
- ☐ Writing - **Research Paper**
- ☐ Culminating Activity
- ☐ **VOCABULARY TERMS TEST** - Weeks 21-24

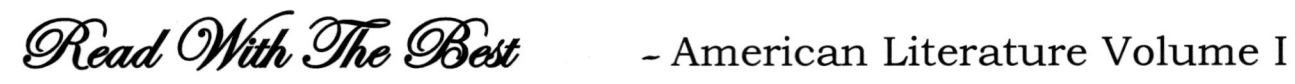

Week 28 **Emily Dickinson**..194-200
*Emily Dickinson - Poems 39, 112, 124, 202, 207, 236, 320, & 340
- ☐ Background Check
- ☐ Words To Know
- ☐ Literary Analysis
- ☐ Critical Reading Questions
- ☐ Make It Real
- ☐ Writing - **Research Paper**
- ☐ Culminating Activity

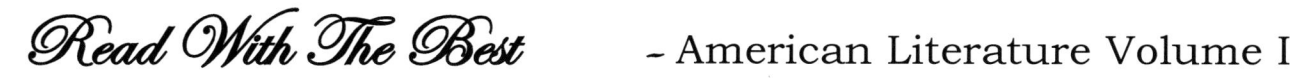

Read With The Best – American Literature Volume I
Table of Contents & Weekly Schedule

Week 29 **Emily Dickinson**..201-206
*Emily Dickinson - Poems 372, 409, 479, 591, 764, 1096, 1773
- [ ] Words To Know
- [ ] Literary Analysis
- [ ] Critical Reading Questions
- [ ] Make It Real
- [ ] Writing - **Research Paper**
- [ ] Culminating Activity

Week 30 **Henry David Thoreau**......*   P825-844.....................................207-212
*Henry David Thoreau - "Resistance to Civil Government" or "Civil Disobedience"
(Try listening to this on librivox.org)
- [ ] Background Check
- [ ] Words To Know
- [ ] Literary Analysis
- [ ] Critical Reading Questions
- [ ] Make It Real
- [ ] Writing - **Research Paper**
- [ ] Culminating Activity

Week 31 **Henry David Thoreau**............ Skip?..213-218
*Henry David Thoreau - Walden: Chapter 1
(Read approximately 9 pages a day. You may choose to listen to this on librivox.org)
- [ ] Literary Analysis
- [ ] Words To Know
- [ ] Critical Reading Questions
- [ ] Make It Real
- [ ] Writing - **Research Paper**
- [ ] Culminating Activity

Week 32 **Henry David Thoreau**............ Skip?..219-224
*Henry David Thoreau - Walden: Chapters 2, 5, 17 & 18
(Read 8 pages a day. You may want to listen to this on librivox.org)
- [ ] Words To Know
- [ ] Critical Reading Questions
- [ ] Make It Real
- [ ] Writing - **Research Paper**
- [ ] Culminating Activity

Read With The Best – American Literature Volume I
Table of Contents & Weekly Schedule

<u>Week 33</u> **Frederick Douglass**..225-232
*Frederick Douglass - Narrative of the Life of Frederick Douglass: Chapters 1-9 (I-IX)
- ☐ Background Check
- ☐ Words To Know
- ☐ Literary Analysis
- ☐ Critical Reading Questions
- ☐ Make It Real
- ☐ Writing - **Expository Essay**
- ☐ Culminating Activity

<u>Week 34</u> **Frederick Douglass**..233-239
*Frederick Douglass - Narrative of the Life of Frederick Douglass: Chapters 10-Appendix (X - Appendix)
- ☐ Words To Know
- ☐ Literary Analysis
- ☐ Critical Reading Questions
- ☐ Make It Real
- ☐ Writing - **Expository Essay**
- ☐ Culminating Activity
- ☐ **Study for LITERARY TERMS TEST** on Week 35 (covering Weeks 25-34)
- ☐ **Study for a VOCABULARY TERMS TEST** on Week 35 (covering Weeks 25-34)

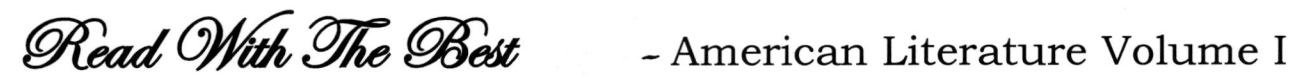

<u>Week 35</u>   **Last Day of Class**
- ☐ **LITERARY TERMS TEST** - Weeks 25-34.
- ☐ **VOCABULARY TERMS TEST** - Weeks 25-34.

Research Paper Check List .... **Appendix**

Vocabulary Terms Tests & Answer Keys

Literary Terms Tests & Answer Keys

CHRISTOPHER COLUMBUS
- LETTER TO SANTANGEL & LETTER TO FERDINAND AND ISABELLA
JOHN SMITH
- FROM *THE GENERAL HISTORY*

WEEK 1

"By prevailing over all obstacles and distractions, one may unfailingly arrive at his chosen goal or destination."

CHRISTOPHER COLUMBUS

BACKGROUND CHECK:

1) How many voyages did Christopher Columbus make? <u>4</u>

2) Did his voyages end successfully and happily? <u>No</u>

3) Which part of the Americas did he discover? <u>West Indies</u>

Name some specific individual countries and islands he discovered.
<u>Haiti, Dominican Republic, Jamaica, Trinidad, South America, Panama</u>

WORDS TO KNOW:

Identify the part of speech of each word, and give one or two synonyms for each.

unfurled	Adj.	unfolded, unwinded
infinity	Noun	beyond, continuity
redress	Noun	aid, amendment
revenue	Noun	acquirement, credit
infirm	Adj.	ailing, anemic
reparation	Noun	adjustment, apology

CHRISTOPHER COLUMBUS
- LETTER TO SANTANGEL & LETTER TO FERDINAND AND ISABELLA

JOHN SMITH
- FROM *THE GENERAL HISTORY*

WEEK 1

CHRISTOPHER COLUMBUS
LITERARY ANALYSIS:

Synecdoche: a figure of speech in which a part stands for the whole such as "Give us this day our daily bread" with bread standing for food.

Personification: Giving human qualities or features to nonhuman objects or abstract ideas.

Example: "The flowers danced in the breeze."

Narration: A type of writing that tells a story by relating a series of connected events. It can include other types of writing such as description.

Point of view: The perspective from which the literary work is presented.

- **First person point of view**: uses the pronoun "I."
- **Second person point of view**: uses the pronoun "you."
- **Third person point of view**: uses the pronouns "he, she, them, it, etc." (Most literary works are written in 3rd person.)
  Related to narration or the way a story is told:
- **Omniscient point of view** (in 3rd person): where the narrator, like God, sees into each character's mind and knows everything that goes on.
- **Limited omniscient point of view** (in 3rd person): where the narrator only has full knowledge of one character (usually the main character).
- **Objective point of view**: where the narrator only reports what a camera would see or what someone would hear the character speak.
- **Stream of consciousness** (in 1st person point of view): where the narrator reveals the inward thoughts of the main character, as the character thinks them. This thinking is often haphazard and illogical.

CHRISTOPHER COLUMBUS
- LETTER TO SANTANGEL & LETTER TO FERDINAND AND ISABELLA

JOHN SMITH
- FROM *THE GENERAL HISTORY*

WEEK 1

CHRISTOPHER COLUMBUS
CRITICAL READING QUESTIONS:

1) How did the people respond when they first saw Columbus? *They fled.*

2) Did the men Columbus sent to search the islands find a king and cities? *No*

3) How did Columbus say he had changed physically during his voyages?
All of the hair on his body was gray, and he was sick.

4) Columbus said he did not go on the voyages to gain *honor* or *wealth*.

5) In the second letter, find an example of synecdoche and personification in the same line. Give an explanation for its usage.
"Heaven have mercy on me, and may the earth weep for me."

Heaven stands for *God.* Earth stands for *People or mankind.*

6) In his letter to the King and Queen concerning the 4th voyage, what does Columbus ask them to do to those who have done wrong? *Punish them.*

After reading about the results of his voyages, do you think he was telling the truth? Why or why not?
Opinion

Christopher Columbus
- Letter to Santangel & Letter to Ferdinand and Isabella

John Smith
- From *The General History*

WEEK 1

"He who does not work, Does not eat."

John Smith

BACKGROUND CHECK:

1) Name some of Smith's adventures before he sailed to the New World.
<u>He cut off the heads of 3 people, served as a foot soldier for the English, was taken as a slave by the Turks, and lived as a pirate.</u>

2) Approximately when was Smith in Virginia? (What dates?) <u>1606-1609</u>
Name 1 other historical figure who lived during this time, or an event that was taking place at this time.
<u>Shakespeare, Queen Elizabeth I, just before King James Bible</u>

3) What role did he first serve in Virginia?
<u>President of Council, Governor of Virginia</u>

4) Why is the account of Smith's rescue by Pocahontas questioned?
<u>He wrote about it for the first time 16 years after it happened.</u>

CHRISTOPHER COLUMBUS
- LETTER TO SANTANGEL & LETTER TO FERDINAND AND ISABELLA
JOHN SMITH
- FROM *THE GENERAL HISTORY*

WEEK 1

JOHN SMITH
BACKGROUND CHECK (CONTINUED):

5) BONUS: What painting hangs in the Rotunda of the Capitol?
A painting of Pocahontas being baptized

What does this say about the story of John Smith? *add Guest not included in painting*
His story is a foundational American story.

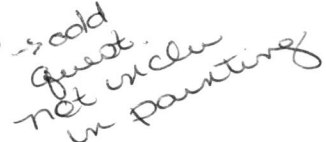

WORDS TO KNOW:

Identify the part of speech of each word, and give one or two synonyms for each.

engrossing	Adj.	absorbing, applying
deposed	Verb	bounced, booted out
untoward	Adj.	adverse, annoying
superfluity	Noun	abundance, excess
derision	Noun	comeback, contempt
ensued	Verb	appeared, attended
conjuration	Noun	magic, sorcery
diverted	Verb	altered, averted
chafed	Verb	abraded, angered, rubbed
mollified	Verb	abated, allayed, soothed
combustion	Noun	agitation, candescence, act or process of burning

CHRISTOPHER COLUMBUS
- LETTER TO SANTANGEL & LETTER TO FERDINAND AND ISABELLA

JOHN SMITH
- FROM *THE GENERAL HISTORY*

WEEK 1

JOHN SMITH
CRITICAL READING QUESTIONS:

1) Even though John Smith writes this account, what person is it written in - 1st, 2nd, or 3rd? *3rd person*

Why do you think he writes it this way?
He wrote this way so that he could present the material as an historian who was emotionally removed from the information.

2) Find at least two sentences that show how Smith trusts God's plan and providence. *Answers will vary.*

3) How are Smith and his men saved from starvation? *The Indians bring food.*

4) Why are John Smith's accounts so significant in American literature?
He is considered the first writer in America.

Read With the Best Diagnostic Prescriptive Services | www.edudps.com

CHRISTOPHER COLUMBUS
- LETTER TO SANTANGEL & LETTER TO FERDINAND AND ISABELLA
JOHN SMITH
- FROM *THE GENERAL HISTORY*

WEEK 1

MAKE IT REAL:

"Columbus sailed the ocean blue, in 1492" -
Make 3 more rhymes to tell what happened on his voyages in 1494, 1498, and 1503.
Answers will vary.

_____

_____

_____

_____

_____

_____

_____

_____

_____

_____

_____

_____

_____

_____

_____

_____

Read With the Best   Diagnostic Prescriptive Services | www.edudps.com

Christopher Columbus
- Letter to Santangel & Letter to Ferdinand and Isabella

John Smith
- From *The General History*

WEEK 1

WRITING ASSIGNMENT:

Pretend that you are a modern day explorer or adventurer such as Columbus or Smith. Fast forward ahead to May, and look back on your school year. Write a descriptive narrative like John Smith or a letter like Christopher Columbus telling about what you accomplished academically, spiritually, physically and socially. Tell about your adventures and set-backs. You may even want to write in 3rd person like John Smith. Try writing in one of the 4 points of view relating to how a story is told. Use descriptive language like Columbus and Smith.

Proof read your paper for grammatical errors and other mistakes.

Christopher Columbus
- Letter to Santangel & Letter to Ferdinand and Isabella

John Smith
- From *The General History*

Week 1

Culminating Activity:

Summarize either the account of Columbus or Smith in your own words and in one of the following points of view: omniscient, limited or objective, or stream of consciousness. Present this orally. In a group setting, you may divide into groups and present it as a group.

JOHN SMITH - FROM *A DESCRIPTION OF NEW ENGLAND*
WILLIAM BRADFORD - FROM *OF PLYMOUTH PLANTATION*

WEEK 2

"History is the memory of time, the life of the dead and the happiness of the living."

JOHN SMITH

WORDS TO KNOW:

Identify the part of speech of each word, and give one or two synonyms for each.

magnanimity	Noun	chivalry, philanthropy, generosity
posterity	Noun	future generations, offspring, descendants
penury	Noun	poverty, destitution
requite	Verb	repay, retaliate, revenge, avenge
dissolute	Adj.	corrupt, debase
recompense	Noun	amends, atonement, restitution

LITERARY ANALYSIS:

Parallel Structure or Parallelism: The use of the same forms of verbs, nouns, or phrases to show emphasis or draw attention in writing. Verbs are used most often in parallel structure.

Example: *"Fred loves reading, writing, and drawing."*

Parallelism is emphasized in English grammar as the correct way to list verbs.

JOHN SMITH - FROM *A DESCRIPTION OF NEW ENGLAND*
WILLIAM BRADFORD - FROM *OF PLYMOUTH PLANTATION*

WEEK 2

JOHN SMITH
CRITICAL READING QUESTIONS:

1) In the opening paragraph of *A Description of New England*, what spiritual reason does Smith give for colonizing New England?
"To convert those poor savages to know Christ and humanity"

Write in your own words the practical reasons he gives.
Reforming unjust, unfair things, starting towns, teaching character, teaching the ignorant, giving jobs to the lazy

2) In the last paragraph, whom is Smith encouraging to come to America?
Fatherless children and young married people

What reasons does he give for them coming?
He says they can become wealthy by laboring in the new land and may also become apprentices.

3) Find two examples of parallel structure in John Smith's use of verbs.
"Erecting towns, peopling countries, informing the ignorant, reforming unjust things, teaching virtue"

"Offend the laws, surfeit with success, burden thy country, abuse thyself, despair in want..."

"Eat, drink, sleep"

JOHN SMITH - FROM *A DESCRIPTION OF NEW ENGLAND*
WILLIAM BRADFORD - FROM *OF PLYMOUTH PLANTATION*

WEEK 2

"All great and honorable actions are accompanied with great difficulties, and both must be enterprised and overcome with answerable courage."

WILLIAM BRADFORD

BACKGROUND CHECK:

1) What political office did Bradford hold in Plymouth Colony?

Governor

2) Why did Bradford come to the New World?

For religious freedom and the cause of separatism

3) Of all Bradford's accomplishments, which one did Cotton Mather think was the most outstanding?

His walk with God

JOHN SMITH - FROM *A DESCRIPTION OF NEW ENGLAND*
WILLIAM BRADFORD - FROM *OF PLYMOUTH PLANTATION*

WEEK 2

WILLIAM BRADFORD
WORDS TO KNOW:

Identify the part of speech of each word, and give one or two synonyms for each.

profane	Adj.	abusive, blasphemous
execrations	Noun	abhorrences, abominations
sundry	Adj.	assorted, different
deliberation	Noun	consideration, discussion, thought
solace	Noun	comfort, relief
victuals	Noun	food, provisions
shallop	Noun	small boat, barge
lusty	Adj.	brawny, dynamic
lustily	Adv.	energetically, forcefully, vigorously, loudly
manifold	Adj.	assorted, multiple
fain	Adj.	eager, inclined, compelled, glad, pleased, willing under the circumstances
mutinous	Adj.	anarchistic, defiant
quelled	Verb	conquered, crush, suppress
beholden	Adj.	bound, grateful
relent	Verb	diminish, decrease, lessen
cozen	Verb	fool, deceive, delude
feigned	Adj.	insincere, artificial, fake
licentiousness	Noun	corruption, debauchery, immorality
quaffing	Verb	guzzling, drinking, gulping
insolent	Adj.	abusive, rude, disrespectful, sassy
lasciviousness	Noun	lustfulness, lewdness, sexually immorality

LITERARY ANALYSIS:

Allusion - A brief reference in a literary work to a famous or well known person, event, or condition.

Example: *Shakespeare uses many Biblical allusions.*

JOHN SMITH - FROM *A DESCRIPTION OF NEW ENGLAND*
WILLIAM BRADFORD - FROM *OF PLYMOUTH PLANTATION*

WEEK 2

WILLIAM BRADFORD
CRITICAL READING QUESTIONS:

1) Did the Pilgrims intend to land at Cape Cod, Massachusetts? *No*
Where were they going? *Virginia*

2) In Chapter (IX) 9, what is ironic about the incident of the accidents of the two young men? What happened to each one? How does Bradford view this?
The profane sailor who was healthy and strong was the first to die on the voyage, and the godly young man was saved miraculously by grabbing a rope after he was thrown overboard. Bradford views this as God's judgment and protection.

3) What did the Pilgrims do when they finally landed?
They fell on their knees and thanked God.

4) How many of the original one hundred passengers on *The Mayflower* survived the first winter? *Around 50 (or one half)*

JOHN SMITH - from *A Description of New England*
WILLIAM BRADFORD - from *Of Plymouth Plantation*

WEEK 2

WILLIAM BRADFORD
CRITICAL READING QUESTIONS (CONTINUED):

5) In Chapter 9, Bradford makes a Greek or Roman classical allusion. Who does he allude to and why?
Seneca; Bradford compares Seneca's very short voyage to the Mayflower's and how God made sure they arrived safely.

6) What is the main theme or idea of this work? Name some examples of this theme that Bradford mentions.
God's providential care; sending the Indians, protection from Indians; "What could now sustain them but the Spirit of God and His Grace?"

7) Why was it necessary to write "The Mayflower Compact"?
Some of the voyagers who were not Separatists or Christians rebelled against the others and said they did not have to obey the previous laws set down because they had not landed in Virginia.

8) When the Pilgrims grew very sick, what stood out about the Christians?
The way they cared for the sick and especially those who had treated them so badly

9) What does Bradford see as the "downfall" of the Plymouth Community?
Prosperity

JOHN SMITH - FROM *A DESCRIPTION OF NEW ENGLAND*
WILLIAM BRADFORD - FROM *OF PLYMOUTH PLANTATION*

WEEK 2

MAKE IT REAL:

In "Dealings With the Natives", try to list the rules outlined in one sentence. Then using these principles, write one sentence outlining rules for getting along with your siblings.

Answers will vary, but the sentence should basically read:

The Indians and Pilgrims are not to harm each other or bring weapons around each other but are to help each other if war is started against them. If someone hurts someone else or steals something, the offender will be punished, and the stolen item should be restored.

JOHN SMITH - FROM *A DESCRIPTION OF NEW ENGLAND*
WILLIAM BRADFORD - FROM *OF PLYMOUTH PLANTATION*

WEEK 2

WRITING ACTIVITY:

Read - "How to Write An Expository Essay" in *Write With The Best Vol. 2*, pages 94 - 95.

This week you will <u>prepare</u> to write an expository essay comparing and contrasting John Smith's historical account and William Bradford's historical account. Make a list of all the similarities and a list of all the differences.

Include theme, point of view, recorded facts, writing styles, use of words, use of argumentation and persuasiveness, etc.

John Smith's historical account	William Bradford's historical account
Similarities	
Differences	

JOHN SMITH - from *A Description of New England*
WILLIAM BRADFORD - from *Of Plymouth Plantation*

WEEK 2

CULMINATING ACTIVITY:

Even though *Of Plymouth Plantation* is an historical account and nonfictional work, it has all the qualities of a successful novel: setting, theme, characters, point of view, conflict, climax or turning point, resolution, and figurative language.

In a classroom setting…

- Divide students in 6 different groups.
- Assign each group 1 of the elements of the novel listed above.
- Give each group 10 minutes to act out the element for the class.

As an individual student…

- Choose 1 or 2 of the elements, and act them out for siblings or parents. (This can be done by presenting a commercial, talk show format, or live news interview.)

JOHN WINTHROP
- "A Model of Christian Charity"
WEEK 3

> *"For we must consider that we shall be a city upon a hill. The eyes of all people are upon us, so that if we shall deal falsely with our God in this work we have undertaken, and so cause Him to withdraw His present help from us, we shall be made a story and a byword through the world..."*

JOHN WINTHROP

BACKGROUND CHECK:

1) Was John Winthrop a Separatist or a Puritan?

A Puritan

Why did he leave England?

Religious restrictions due to the reign of Charles I, economic unrest, and lack of employment

2) How many years after William Bradford died, did John Winthrop settle in Massachusetts?

9-10 years later

3) What was Winthrop's settlement called?

Massachusetts Bay Colony

4) What profession did Winthrop have in England?

Lawyer

John Winthrop
– "A Model of Christian Charity"
Week 3

WORDS TO KNOW:

Identify the part of speech of each word, and give one or two synonyms for each.

rent	Verb	tear, separate, break
moderating	Verb	abating, allaying, restraining, calming
superfluities	Noun	abundances, excesses
subsistence	Noun	existence, reality, duration, resources
sloth	Noun	idleness, inactivity, laziness
voluptuousness	Noun	provocativeness, sensuousness, luxuriousness
pittance	Noun	allowance, small amount
posterity	Noun	lineage, offspring, seed, descendants
contiguous	Adj.	abutting, adjoining, adjacent, beside
infuse	Verb	permeate, implant
repining	Verb	fretting, grumping, wishing, moaning
reproaching	Verb	abusing, admonishing, upbraid, insult
dissimilitude	Noun	contrast, discrepancy
propensity	Noun	ability, aptness
requital	Noun	compensation, payment, retaliation, retribution
perjured	Verb	deceived, deluded, lied, misled

LITERARY ANALYSIS:

Metaphor - A comparison of two things without the use of the words "like" or "as."

Example: *Jesus said, "I am the bread of life."*

Tone - The author's attitude toward his subject. Tone can be serious, sarcastic, realistic, depressing, romantic, or adventurous.

John Winthrop
- "A Model of Christian Charity"
Week 3

CRITICAL READING QUESTIONS:

1) Name 3 Biblical allusions Winthrop makes. Next to each allusion, write the point he is making with the allusion.
Answers will vary – there are several Old Testament allusions.
___
___
___

2) What are the two traits Winthrop says must be used by community members in the way they deal with each other? *Justice and mercy*

3) What transition words does Winthrop use repeatedly at the beginning of new paragraphs or thoughts to outline his points?
"First," "secondly," "thirdly" and sometimes "fourthly" or "lastly"

4) Name two metaphors Winthrop uses to compare and describe the Christian community. *The human body and a city on a hill*

5) What Biblical example of friendship and love does Winthrop use to persuade his readers? *David and Jonathan*

6) What word does Winthrop use to describe the community's relationship with God, insisting that it cannot be broken, or they will be severely punished? *A covenant*

7) What tone does Winthrop use in this essay? *Serious and grave*

8) In the beginning of the essay, what subject is his focus? *Giving money and lending*

9) Whose words does Winthrop use in his final paragraph to exhort the brethren to obey? *Moses*

John Winthrop
- "A Model of Christian Charity"

Week 3

MAKE IT REAL:

Winthrop's "city upon a hill" metaphor is very famous and has been used in many famous speeches for decades.
Winthrop is referring to Matthew 5: 14-15 when he uses the metaphor. Find at least 2 examples where this metaphor is used in famous writings, and explain why each specific writer is using it. What does it mean in each example?

<u>*You can find this metaphor or indirect references to it in almost every presidential inaugural speech since Lincoln. Specifically, Ronald Reagan & John F. Kennedy used it in their inaugural speeches.*</u>

_____

_____

_____

_____

_____

_____

_____

_____

_____

_____

_____

_____

_____

_____

_____

_____

JOHN WINTHROP
- "A MODEL OF CHRISTIAN CHARITY"

WEEK 3

WRITING ASSIGNMENT:

Using *Write With The Best Vol. 2*, pages 37-42, you will write an expository essay comparing and contrasting John Smith's historical account with William Bradford's. Refer to the chart you made last week. You will need to write a brief topical outline to organize your paragraph. See Unit 3 for directions on devising an outline. Many of you may have never written an essay before, so be sure to follow the guidelines given in Unit 4 of *Write With The Best Vol. 2* (You will need to read through the unit carefully). Proofread your essay using the checklist on page 108, and remember to refer to pages 94-95 for tips on writing this essay.

John Winthrop
- "A Model of Christian Charity"

Week 3

Culminating Activity:

Pick three of your vocabulary words from this week, and create a sentence that makes sense using all three. Try to write a sentence about Winthrop's essay "A Model of Christian Charity." In a classroom, students can be divided into groups to do this.

ANNE BRADSTREET

"THE PROLOGUE", "BEFORE THE BIRTH OF ONE OF HER CHILDREN", "HERE FOLLOWS SOME VERSES UPON THE BURNING OF OUR HOUSE" AND "TO MY DEAR AND LOVING HUSBAND", "THE AUTHOR TO HER BOOK", AND "TO MY DEAR CHILDREN"

WEEK 4

> *"Thou ill-formed offspring of my feeble brain,*
> *Who after birth didst by my side remain,*
> *Till snatched from thence*
> *by friends, less wise than true,*
> *Who thee abroad, exposed to public view."*

ANNE BRADSTREET

BACKGROUND CHECK:

1) What kind of education did Bradstreet receive? *A superior education – different from most women of her time*

2) How many children did she have? *8*

3) Did she publish her own works? *No, her brother-in-law did.*

4) Why is her poetry so significant? *Her book of poems was the first published volume of poems written by a citizen of the New World.*

LITERARY ANALYSIS:

Iambic Couplet: two successive lines of poetry that rhyme and have a rhythmic pattern of an unaccented syllable followed by an accented syllable. It is one of the most often used forms of English verse. Example: "Within this Tomb a Patriot lies / That was both pious, just and wise."

Conceit: a comparison of two unlikely and sometimes farfetched things that is drawn out within the entire poem. A conceit is a type of metaphor.

ANNE BRADSTREET

"The Prologue", "Before the Birth of One of Her Children", "Here Follows Some Verses Upon the Burning of Our House" and "To My Dear And Loving Husband", "The Author to Her Book", and "To My Dear Children"

Week 4

"The Prologue"
Words To Know:

Identify the part of speech of each word, and give one or two synonyms for each.

mean	Adj.	poor; of or in inferior circumstances, base, beggarly, common
overfluent	Adj.	abundant
consort	Noun / Verb	associate, partner, companion / fraternize, accompany, associate
irreparable	Adj.	broken, destroyed, beyond repair, hopeless
requital [see Winthrop]	Noun	revenge, recompense, retaliation
maxim	Noun	saying, adage, axiom, belief
obnoxious	Adj.	annoying, disagreeable, offensive, repulsive
carping	Adj.	complaining, critical, criticizing, disparaging
feigned [see Winthrop]	Verb	pretended, acted, assumed, bluffed
precedency	Noun	precedence, antecedence, ante position, lead
quills	Noun	feathers, instruments, pens
deign	Verb	lower oneself, condescend, consent

Critical Reading Questions:

1) How does the author feel about her own writing?

She thinks she will never be a good writer because she lacks the skill.

2) What is the best meaning of stanza 4?

Even though the Greek poet could not speak correctly, he wrote beautiful poetry.

3) Name 2 allusions in this poem. *Muses, Bartos, Demosthenes, Calliope*

4) What does Bradstreet say about men? *Men are superior to women.*

5) In stanza 5, what does she think others will say about her poetry?

People will say her poetry is stolen or well-written by chance only.

ANNE BRADSTREET

WEEK 4

- "THE PROLOGUE", "BEFORE THE BIRTH OF ONE OF HER CHILDREN", "HERE FOLLOWS SOME VERSES UPON THE BURNING OF OUR HOUSE" AND "TO MY DEAR AND LOVING HUSBAND", "THE AUTHOR TO HER BOOK", AND "TO MY DEAR CHILDREN"

"BEFORE THE BIRTH OF ONE OF HER CHILDREN"
WORDS TO KNOW:

Identify the part of speech of each word, and give one or two synonyms for each.

irrevocable	Adj.	fixed, unchangeable, certain
interred	Verb	buried, entombed, planted, covered up
stepdame	Noun	stepmother
hearse	Noun	coffin, support for burial, grave
oblivious	Adj.	unaware, ignorant, absent

CRITICAL READING QUESTIONS:

1) Who is this poem addressed to? *Anne Bradstreet's husband*

2) Why do you think Bradstreet is writing this poem?
She thinks she may die in childbirth.

3) What does she mean by "the sentence past is irrevocable, a common thing, yet oh, inevitable"?
When God chooses for someone to die, it cannot be changed; death will finally come to all.

4) What does Bradstreet want her husband to do with her children if she dies?
Take care of her remaining children and keep them from a mean stepmother

5) What does Bradstreet want her husband to do with her faults when she dies? With her good qualities?
Faults – bury them with her and forget them
Virtues – keep in his memory

ANNE BRADSTREET

- "THE PROLOGUE", "BEFORE THE BIRTH OF ONE OF HER CHILDREN", "HERE FOLLOWS SOME VERSES UPON THE BURNING OF OUR HOUSE" AND "TO MY DEAR AND LOVING HUSBAND", "THE AUTHOR TO HER BOOK", AND "TO MY DEAR CHILDREN"

WEEK 4

"HERE FOLLOWS SOME VERSES UPON THE BURNING OF OUR HOUSE" AND "TO MY DEAR AND LOVING HUSBAND"

WORDS TO KNOW:

Identify the part of speech of each word and give one or two synonyms for each.

succorless	Adj.	helpless, destitute
repine	Verb	fret, complain, lament, languish, moan
bereft	Adj.	lacking, missing, beggared, deprived
adieu	Noun	farewell, goodbye, parting, so-long
recompense	Noun	something returned, paid back, amends, atonement
manifold	Adj.	abundant, many, assorted, complex

CRITICAL READING QUESTIONS:

1) Where in the poem "Upon the Burning" does Bradstreet remind herself not to have too much affection for earthly things? **Starting at line 16**

2) What is Bradstreet's attitude about her house being burnt? Where is her "house on high"? **She is resigned to it because she knows her treasure is above and not on earth; heaven**

3) Who is the mighty Architect? **God**
This is an example of what literary term? **a metaphor**

4) What form of English verse is "To My Dear" and "Upon the Burning of Our House"? **Iambic couplet**

5) List in your own words four declarations that Bradstreet makes about her love for her husband. **He and she are one flesh, he is deeply loved, she is very happy with him, his love is worth more than gold and riches.**
There may be additional answers also.

Read With the Best   Diagnostic Prescriptive Services | www.edudps.com

Anne Bradstreet

Week 4

- "The Prologue", "Before the Birth of One of Her Children", "Here Follows Some Verses Upon the Burning of Our House" and "To My Dear And Loving Husband", "The Author to Her Book", and "To My Dear Children"

"The Author to Her Book" and "To My Dear Children"
Words To Know:

Identify the part of speech of each word, and give one or two synonyms for each.

trudge	Verb	walk heavily, clump, march, plod
visage	Noun	appearance, aspect, countenance, features
nought	Noun	nothing, none
bequeath	Verb	bestow, commit, devise, endow
carnal	Adj.	savage, vulgar, abominable, barbarous
follies	Noun	nonsenses, absurdities, craziness
consumption	Noun	use, devouring, consuming, damage, decay
travail	Noun	struggle, agony, anguish
felicity	Noun	happiness, bliss, contentment
verity	Noun	truth, accuracy, veracity
maugre	Noun	ill-will, spite
circumspection	Noun	caution, carefulness, discretion
untoward	Adj.	(See Week 1) troublesome, adverse, contrary

ANNE BRADSTREET

"The Prologue", "Before the Birth of One of Her Children", "Here Follows Some Verses Upon the Burning of Our House" and "To My Dear And Loving Husband", "The Author to Her Book", and "To My Dear Children"

WEEK 4

"The Author to Her Book" and "To My Dear Children"

CRITICAL READING QUESTIONS:

1) What is the "ill-formed offspring of my feeble brain" in *"The Author to Her Book"*?
<u>Her book of poems, *The Tenth Muse*</u>

2) In line 2 and throughout the poem, what kind of relationship does Bradstreet say she has with her book?   <u>Mother and child</u>
What literary term is this called? <u>conceit</u>
What other figure of speech does Bradstreet use when describing the book as a child?
<u>personification</u>

3) What is the occasion of her writing this poem?
<u>The publication of her book without her knowledge</u>

4) Name 3 ways Bradstreet compares her book to a child – list actions or words.
<u>"Washed thy face," "Stretched thy joints," "Dressed him better"</u>

5) Why does Bradstreet say she is writing the letter *"To My Dear Children"*?
<u>That they may gain spiritual advantage by her experience</u>

6) Why did God send afflictions to Bradstreet?
<u>So she will see her sin and make things right</u>
Name some of these afflictions.
<u>personal sickness, financial problems, sickness of children, weakness, doubts and fears</u>

7) To Bradstreet, what makes heaven or hell? <u>The presence or absence of God</u>

Anne Bradstreet

"The Prologue", "Before the Birth of One of Her Children", "Here Follows Some Verses Upon the Burning of Our House" and "To My Dear And Loving Husband", "The Author to Her Book", and "To My Dear Children"

Week 4

Make It Real:

Read *"To My Dear and Loving Husband"* out loud while you clap on the accented syllables. Then read *"Upon the Burning of Our House"* while you clap on the accented syllables. This will help you see the rhythm of the iambic pattern.

Writing Assignment:

Choose a domestic subject such as child-rearing or marriage or an occurrence or incident (such as death), and write a brief poem using iambic couplets like Bradstreet. Also, try to use the number of words she used in each line so that you can use iambic pentameter.

Proofread your poem.

_____

_____

_____

_____

_____

_____

_____

_____

_____

_____

_____

_____

_____

ANNE BRADSTREET

"THE PROLOGUE", "BEFORE THE BIRTH OF ONE OF HER CHILDREN", "HERE FOLLOWS SOME VERSES UPON THE BURNING OF OUR HOUSE" AND "TO MY DEAR AND LOVING HUSBAND", "THE AUTHOR TO HER BOOK", AND "TO MY DEAR CHILDREN"

WEEK 4

CULMINATING ACTIVITY:

Assign one of Bradstreet's four poems from this week [except *"Prologue"*] to each group. [Individual students should choose one poem and have someone read it out loud for them.] While one person reads the poem out loud, others in the group should act out [by pantomime, no words] the words being spoken. Hand gestures and body motions can be used. Students in groups need to read over the poem together first, and make sure they understand it completely.

MARY ROWLANDSON
- FROM *A NARRATIVE OF THE CAPTIVITY AND RESTORATION OF MRS. MARY ROWLANDSON*

WEEK 5

MARY ROWLANDSON

"Yet I see, when God calls a person to anything, and through never so many difficulties, yet He is fully able to carry them through and make them see, and say they have been gainers thereby."

BACKGROUND CHECK:

1) What was the name of the series of battles that began in 1675?
King Phillip's War

2) Name at least 3 possible reasons for this war.
Execution of tribesmen, starvation of Indians, resistance to expansion of colonists

3) Who was Mary Rowlandson?
A minister's wife from Lancaster

4) What were the "removes" she spoke of?
Movings from place to place

MARY ROWLANDSON
← FROM *A NARRATIVE OF THE CAPTIVITY AND RESTORATION OF MRS. MARY ROWLANDSON*

WEEK 5

WORDS TO KNOW:

Identify the part of speech of each word, and give one or two synonyms for each.

daunt	Verb	frighten, alarm, baffle
din	Noun	loud, continuous noise, bedlam, clamor
disconsolate	Adj.	depressed, unhappy, crestfallen
trumpery	Noun	deception, nonsense, rubbish
doleful, dolefulest	Adj.	depressing, afflicted, (dolefulest- most doleful)
hallowed	Adj.	holy, revered, blessed, consecrated
infidel	Noun	nonbeliever, agnostic, atheist, heretic
lamentable	Adj.	upsetting, miserable, calamitous, awful
melancholic	Adj.	depressed, sad, despondent, dejected
insolency	Noun	disrespect, disregard, contempt
providence	Noun	thrift, foresight, guidance
requited	Verb	compensated, paid, recompensed
incivility	Noun	discourtesy, disrespect, rudeness
bereft	Adj.	lacking, missing, destitute, deprived
scoff (verb)	Verb	belittle, deride, discount, make fun of
scourge	Noun	plague, torment, affliction, correction, curse
recompense	Noun / Verb	atonement, compensation, payment, / atone, balance, compensate
dispensation	Noun	allotment, appointment, award
abated	Verb	allayed, lessened, diminished

LITERARY ANALYSIS:

Simile: A comparison of two or more things using the words "like" or "as."

Genre: The kind or type of a work of literature. Genres in literature include novels, sonnets, short stories, etc.

MARY ROWLANDSON
FROM *A NARRATIVE OF THE CAPTIVITY AND RESTORATION OF MRS. MARY ROWLANDSON*

WEEK 5

CRITICAL READING QUESTIONS:

1) How does Mary Rowlandson establish her reliability as an author and narrator in the first few lines of the narrative?
She gives the exact dates and number of the captives taken.

2) What wound does Mary receive as she runs from the house?
She receives a bullet wound in the side.

3) Mary had previously thought and stated that she would rather die than what?
Be captured alive by Indians

4) How does Mary's six year old daughter die?
Malnourishment and her wounds

5) What do the Indians do with her daughter's body?
They bury her.

6) How does Mary say God is merciful to her after the death of her child?
He keeps her from taking her own life.

7) What was the name of the Englishman that came with ransom money for Mary? Who paid the ransom money?
Mr. John Hoar; the people from Boston

8) How long was Mary in captivity?
11 weeks and 5 days

MARY ROWLANDSON
- FROM *A NARRATIVE OF THE CAPTIVITY AND RESTORATION OF MRS. MARY ROWLANDSON*

WEEK 5

CRITICAL READING QUESTIONS (CONTINUED):

9) What is the theme of her narrative?
The sovereignty, faithfulness, and goodness of God

10) Name at least 3 major and marvelous ways that God shows his Providence in Mary's life during her captivity.
God sends her a Bible which sustains her; she is given favor with King Phillip; she is not killed or did not die from her wound; she does not kill herself; Captain Beer showed her how to heal her wound and many more. Answers will vary.

11) How does Mary say her affliction helped her?
Her affliction helped her to see the vanity of outward things such as health, wealth, and friends and that her entire dependence must be upon God alone.

12) Why do you think this narrative became one of the most popular literary works of the seventeenth century and its genre the first in American literature?
It had all the elements of a great novel – adventure, heroism, action, and a good ending.

13) Name the genre of Mary Rowlandson's account.
Captivity narrative

MARY ROWLANDSON
– FROM *A NARRATIVE OF THE CAPTIVITY AND RESTORATION OF MRS. MARY ROWLANDSON*

WEEK 5

MAKE IT REAL:

We are all like Mary Rowlandson in that we all have choices about how we will deal with our circumstances, but most of our afflictions do not compare to hers in any way.
Think about what might have happened to Mary if she had not have responded to her trials in the way she did.
Write a brief paragraph in first person with Mary as the narrator, in which you describe a different attitude and the results of this attitude (things that happened).
Answers will vary.

MARY ROWLANDSON
– FROM *A NARRATIVE OF THE CAPTIVITY AND RESTORATION OF MRS. MARY ROWLANDSON*

WEEK 5

WRITING ASSIGNMENT:

Now that you have read Anne Bradstreet's account of her life "To My Dear Children" and Mary Rowlandson's *Narrative*, using what you learned last week about iambic couplets and conceits and other weeks about metaphors and similes, write another poem in iambic couplets about Bradstreet's and Rowlandson's view on Christian affliction and suffering.
Try to use a conceit (extended metaphor) like Bradstreet did in "The Author to Her Book." At least use descriptive language and at least one simile.
Proofread your poem.
(You can refer to *Write With The Best, Vol.1* for additional help in writing poetry if you have this book.)

_____

_____

_____

_____

_____

_____

_____

_____

_____

_____

_____

_____

MARY ROWLANDSON
‑ FROM *A NARRATIVE OF THE CAPTIVITY AND RESTORATION OF MRS. MARY ROWLANDSON*

WEEK 5

CULMINATING ACTIVITY:

As an individual or in classroom groups, see how many similes and metaphors can be found in Mary Rowlandson's *Narrative*. Give a time limit of 10-15 minutes.

COTTON MATHER
- FROM *THE WONDERS OF THE INVISIBLE WORLD*

WEEK 6

COTTON MATHER

"Now, by these confessions 'tis agreed that the devil has made a dreadful knot of witches in the country, and by the help of witches has dreadfully increased that knot."

BACKGROUND CHECK:

1) At what age did Mather attend college, and what college did he attend?
Harvard at age 12

2) How many of his literary works were published? *400*

3) How did he follow in his father's footsteps? *He became a pastor.*

4) What earned Mather a significant place in American literature?
His work as an historian

5) Mather lived during what famous event in early American history?
The Salem Witch Trials

COTTON MATHER
- FROM *THE WONDERS OF THE INVISIBLE WORLD*

WEEK 6

WORDS TO KNOW:

Identify the part of speech of each word, and give one or two synonyms for each.

extirpation	Noun	extermination, annihilation, destruction
boughs	Noun	branches, arms, limbs, shoots
halcyon	Adj.	gentle, calm, peaceful, balmy, harmonious
malefactor	Noun	con, convict, culprit, criminal, delinquent
diabolism,	Noun	witchcraft, sorcery, black magic, demonianism
diabolically	Adv.	brutally, cruelly, demonically
spectral	Adj.	ghostly, eerie, haunted
sundry	Adj.	assorted, miscellaneous, manifold, different
preternatural	Adj.	aberrant, different, unusual, atypical, anomalous
concernment	Noun	importance, concern, consequence, relevance
prodigious	Adj.	extraordinary, fabulous, abnormal, amazing, astounding
deposed	Verb	booted out, bounced, broke, degraded, dismissed
variance	Noun	difference, argument, contention, conflict
apprehension	Noun	alarm, disquiet, concern, anxiety, fear
incarnate	Adj.	embodied, human, exteriorized, physical, real
specter	Noun	ghost, apparition, appearance, demon

LITERARY ANALYSIS:

Anaphora - The repetition of the same words at the beginning of successive phrases.

Example: The Beatitudes: "Blessed are the poor….," "Blessed are they that mourn…."

COTTON MATHER
– From *The Wonders of the Invisible World*

WEEK 6

CRITICAL READING QUESTIONS:

1) Why does Mather think the Devil is bothering New England?
The Devil is disturbed because of the work of God in New England, and he wants to destroy the religious community.

2) What is the "vine" that God has planted? What other references to plants and trees did Mather make? What figure of speech is this?
The vine that God has planted is the colony of Massachusetts and the Puritan work there; deep root, boughs, branches; the vine is a metaphor.

3) Was Mather present at any of the witch trials? *No*

4) Has he recorded the trial details as an historian or advocate of the trials?
An historian

5) What example of anaphora does Mather use in the first lines of "The Wonders" to describe the attempt the Devil is making upon the people of New England?
"An attempt more difficult, more surprising, more snarled…" or "among the Ephesians, among…"

COTTON MATHER
– FROM *THE WONDERS OF THE INVISIBLE WORLD*

WEEK 6

MAKE IT REAL:

After Cotton Mather died, much of the Puritan ideal died with him, and many changes took place in the eighteenth century. Mather saw the Salem Witch Trials as a ploy of the Devil to end the Puritan ideal. What is your opinion of the Witch Trials and Mather's view of it? Write your opinion in one sentence. Try to use anaphora in your sentence.
Answers will vary.

COTTON MATHER
– From *The Wonders of the Invisible World*

WEEK 6

WRITING ASSIGNMENT:

You will begin this week to learn how to write a persuasive essay. Using Mather's short essay from *The Wonders of the Invisible World*, complete the exercises from Days 1-3 in *Write With the Best, Volume 2,* pages 29-34.
Instead of using Thomas Paine's essay in *Write With the Best*, you will be using the essay by Cotton Mather you read this week to complete the exercises in *Write With the Best*.

Thesis Statement:
"…And it may easily be supposed that the devil was exceedingly disturbed, when he perceived such a people here accomplishing the promise of old made unto our blessed Jesus, that He should have the utmost parts of the earth for His possession" or "I believe that never were more satanical devices used for the unsettling of any people under the sun…"

Attention Grabber:
Example of the uproar of the Ephesians in the Bible

Arguments to support thesis statement:

1) A malefactor convicted of murder and witchcraft told of a plot against this area.

2) Examples of spectral exhibitions

3) Twenty-one have confessed to witchcraft and signed the Devil's book.

4) Witch meetings have been held to find methods of rooting out the Christian religion from this country.

Lasting final thought in concluding paragraph:
"You are to take the truth, just as it was; and the truth will hurt no good man."

COTTON MATHER
– From *The Wonders of the Invisible World*

CULMINATING ACTIVITY:

Alone or as a group, conduct a news interview with Cotton Mather, and report his facts about the witch trial. Remember that he was not present, so he will be reporting what he has heard only. You may choose to use a reporter and other witnesses also.

EDWARD TAYLOR - "Huswifery"
JONATHAN EDWARDS - "Sinners in the Hands of an Angry God"

WEEK 7

EDWARD TAYLOR

"Make me, O Lord, thy Spinning Wheel Complete."

BACKGROUND CHECK:

1) What were some of the professions of Edward Taylor?

Minister, physician, teacher

2) When were Taylor's poems discovered?

1930's

3) Taylor's poetry reflects a lot of what kind of dialect of his upbringing?

Farming dialect

WORDS TO KNOW:

Identify the part of speech of each word, and give one or two synonyms for each.

distaff	Noun	the staff on which the wool or flax is wound before spinning
reel	Verb	wobble, falter, stagger
varnished	Verb	embellished, adorned, decorated, covered
Fulling Mills	Noun	a mill for fulling cloth

EDWARD TAYLOR - "Huswifery"
JONATHAN EDWARDS - "Sinners in the Hands of an Angry God"

WEEK 7

LITERARY ANALYSIS:

Imagery: A sensory detail the author uses to paint word pictures in the mind of the reader.
Imagery appeals to any or all of the five senses and can include similes, metaphors, and other figurative language.

Metaphysical Conceit: An extended metaphor that uses lofty, elaborate and often intellectual and philosophical language. It also uses many highly imaginative images and intense emotion.
(John Donne and George Herbert are famous British metaphysical poets, and Edward Taylor and T.S. Eliot are considered American metaphysical poets.)

CRITICAL READING QUESTIONS:

1) What imagery is sustained throughout this poem?

Spinning wheel, sewing / knitting, and clothing

2) List the 3 processes of spinning thread that Taylor develops in each stanza.

Making the thread, weaving the cloth, making a garment

3) The extended metaphor in this poem is called a what?

A metaphysical conceit

What two unlikely things is Taylor comparing in this poem?

The comparison is between cloth making/ spinning and God's Grace or Salvation.

4) In your own words, write a short paraphrase of Taylor's prayer to God. It does not have to be in poetic form.

Answers will vary

EDWARD TAYLOR - "HUSWIFERY"
JONATHAN EDWARDS - "SINNERS IN THE HANDS OF AN ANGRY GOD"

WEEK 7

"There is nothing that keeps wicked men at any one moment out of hell, but the mere pleasure of God."

JONATHAN EDWARDS

BACKGROUND CHECK:

1) The men in Jonathan Edwards' family were what profession?
Ministers, pastors, and preachers

2) Where was Edwards educated the first 12 years of his life? *At home*

3) How many siblings did he have? *11* How many children did Edwards have? *11*

4) Where did Edwards go at age 13? *To Yale University*

5) What was Edwards' goal for his congregation?
To restore to them a sense of religious commitment and transform them from mere intellectual believers to converted Christians

6) What was the revival called that took place for 15 years during Edwards' time?
The Great Awakening

7) (You will have to do research to answer this question) How did Edwards preach "Sinners in the Hands of an Angry God"? *He read it monotone*
How did people respond? *the congregation wept, screamed, and some fainted.*

Read With the Best — Diagnostic Prescriptive Services | www.edudps.com

EDWARD TAYLOR - "HUSWIFERY"
JONATHAN EDWARDS - "SINNERS IN THE HANDS OF AN ANGRY GOD"

WEEK 7

JONATHAN EDWARDS

WORDS TO KNOW:

Identify the part of speech of each word, and give one or two synonyms for each.

manifold	Adj.	abundant, many, assorted, diverse
contrivance	Noun	plan, fabrication, angle, design
incensed	Adj.	angered, bothered, exasperated.
potent	Adj.	effective, powerful, forceful, authoritative
dolorous	Adj.	miserable, anguished, afflicted, dire
arbitrary	Adj.	whimsical, chance, approximate, erratic, capricious
immoderate	Adj.	excessive, extreme, exaggerated, enormous
prudence	Noun	caution, austerity, care
liableness	Noun	aptness, obliged
enmity	Noun	hatred, animosity, acrimony
abate	Verb	lessen, allay, cool
unobliged	Adj.	not obliged, unhelpful, disobedient
ineffable	Adj.	celestial, divine, ethereal, too great for words
mitigation	Noun	alleviation, reduction, cure, relief
lamentable	Adj.	upsetting, miserable, awful, calamitous

*In a sentence, use three of these words to describe Edwards' sermon or the effects of it.
(Answers will vary.)

EDWARD TAYLOR - "HUSWIFERY"
JONATHAN EDWARDS - "SINNERS IN THE HANDS OF AN ANGRY GOD"

WEEK 7

JONATHAN EDWARDS
CRITICAL READING QUESTIONS:

1) Find at least 3 similes or metaphors Edwards uses to make his point.
The wrath of God is like great waters, wickedness as heavy as lead, as great heaps of chaff before the whirlwind, arrows of death, wrath burns like fire, like greedy hungry lions, like the chaff, God's wrath are black clouds, God's wrath is a bent bow, as one holds a spider over a fire, like a thread, a lake of burning brimstone, etc.

2) What reason does Edwards give for God not already striking down the wicked or smiting them in His wrath?
The (sovereign) pleasure of God or His Will; His appointed time has not come.

3) What metaphor does Edwards use to describe the wrath of God in "Application" in paragraph five?
A bow ready to be shot

4) Find an example of personification.
"Hell opens its mouth wide", "The pit has opened its mouth under them", "Justice calls out", "Creation groans with you" – Answers may vary, but may include these.

5) What intense and sharp images and similes does Edwards use in "Application", the end of paragraph 3 to persuade his readers? What senses does he appeal to? Why do you think Edwards uses a lot of "nature" imagery?
A terrible storm and whirlwind with black clouds, thunder, and rough winds; Sight, hearing, touch; He uses nature imagery because his readers can relate to it.

EDWARD TAYLOR - "HUSWIFERY"
JONATHAN EDWARDS - "SINNERS IN THE HANDS OF AN ANGRY GOD"

WEEK 7

JONATHAN EDWARDS

CRITICAL READING QUESTIONS (CONTINUED):

6) Where in the sermon does Edwards start to become personal and speak to his audience as "you"? What does he say is the use of this awful subject?

In "Application"; to awaken unconverted persons

7) What is a sinner compared to while God holds him over the fires of hell? *A spider*
Draw a picture to illustrate this.

8) What does Edwards ask of his audience in the last paragraph?

To fly from the wrath of God

9) What is the tone of this writing?

Somber, grave, serious, exhorting, blount, dramatic

Were all of Edwards' writings written in this tone?

No – he also wrote about God's mercy.

Edward Taylor - "Huswifery"
Jonathan Edwards - "Sinners in the Hands of an Angry God"

Week 7

Make It Real:

What do you think would happen if Edwards' sermon was preached this Sunday in your church or your neighbor's church? Write a sentence using imagery to answer this question. How would it be received? How much do you hear others talk about the wrath of God, and how much do you talk about it? How much is the wrath of God talked about in the Bible? Try to estimate the percentage of verses about the wrath of God in the Bible.

__Answers will vary. The percentage of verses or topics about the wrath of God in the Bible is estimated around 60%.__

Edward Taylor - "Huswifery"
Jonathan Edwards - "Sinners in the Hands of an Angry God"

Week 7

Writing Assignment:

This week you will practice writing outlines again. Read pages 87-90 carefully in *Write With the Best, Vol. 2*. Write a sentence outline for "Sinners in the Hands of an Angry God" (the first part only, not "Application"). Also, write a thesis statement for it, and place it at the top of your outline. Check your outline by using the Proofreading Checklist on page 106

EDWARD TAYLOR - "HUSWIFERY"
JONATHAN EDWARDS - "SINNERS IN THE HANDS OF AN ANGRY GOD"

WEEK 7

CULMINATING ACTIVITY:

Teachers will refer to the answers for number 1 under Jonathan Edwards – "Critical Reading," and assign each group one simile or metaphor from "Sinners in the Hands of an Angry God" to act out for the other students (or family members). (This can be done through charades or verbal acting.) The other students are to guess which specific imagery, simile, or metaphor the group is acting out.

BENJAMIN FRANKLIN
- THE AUTOBIOGRAPHY OF BENJAMIN FRANKLIN
WEEK 8

> *"Having emerged from the poverty and obscurity in which I was born and bred, to a state of affluence and some degree of reputation in the world, and having gone so far through life with a considerable share of felicity, the conducing means I made use of, which, with the blessing of God, so well succeeded, my posterity may like to know."*

BENJAMIN FRANKLIN

BACKGROUND CHECK:

1) What profession did Franklin's father plan on him having?

A minister

2) What profession did Franklin's brother have, to which Franklin himself was apprenticed?

A printer

3) Name four of Franklin's best accomplishments.

Founded first library, invented a stove, wrote Poor Richard's Almanac, served as a delegate to Constitutional Convention, helped write Declaration of Independence, started University of Pennsylvania, discovered the laws of electricity, invented bifocals, etc.

BENJAMIN FRANKLIN
- *THE AUTOBIOGRAPHY OF BENJAMIN FRANKLIN*

WEEK 8

WORDS TO KNOW:

Identify the part of speech of each word, and give one or two synonyms for each.

accost	Verb	approach, address, confront, appeal to
scrivener	Noun	columnist, commentator, contributor, professional writer, someone who drafts documents
affable	Adj.	friendly, amiable, amicable, benevolent, congenial, cordial
approbation	Noun	praise, admiration, approval, consent, esteem
fractious	Adj.	grouchy, cross, awkward, crabby, captious
frugality	Noun	economizing, avarice, conservation, prudence
inducements	Noun	incentives, motives, attractions, causes
conventicle	Noun	a secret unauthorized meeting for religious worship or a building for religious assembly
apparitor	Noun	an officer of civil servant
libeler	Noun	defamer
quagmire	Noun	bad situation, dilemma, difficulty, predicament
dissuade	Verb	talk out of, advise against, deter, deprecate, exhort, divert, caution against
diffidence	Noun	hesitancy, lack of confidence, constraint, doubt, fear
eminent	Adj.	very important, famous, august, celebrated, elevated, dominant
errata	Noun	error, misprint, corrigenda
lampoon	Noun	parody, satire, caricature, invective
parsimony	Noun	stinginess, frugality, miserliness, selfishness
donundrum	Noun	puzzle, enigma, mystery, brain-teaser, puzzlement, problem
disputations	Noun	controversies, disputes, debates, dissensions

LITERARY ANALYSIS:

Diction: The style of speaking and writing reflected in the choice and use of words. It also refers to the arrangement of words in statements and the emphasis with which they are spoken.

BENJAMIN FRANKLIN
- THE AUTOBIOGRAPHY OF BENJAMIN FRANKLIN

WEEK 8

CRITICAL READING QUESTIONS:

1) Whom does Franklin write the first part of his autobiography to? *His son William*

2) In the first paragraph of his autobiography, Franklin says he has achieved what three goals after coming from poverty and obscurity? *Affluence, reputation, and felicity*

3) Why does Franklin say he is writing the autobiography?
He thinks some of his posterity may want to imitate some of the things he did in life, that his son would learn of his life, to indulge his vanity

Whom does he say he owes thanks to for the happiness of his life? *God*

4) What religion was Franklin's family during the Reformation? *Protestants*

5) At the beginning of the autobiography, Franklin says he cannot relive his life, so he will do the next best thing. What is this?
Remembering and telling about his life by writing about it

6) Did Franklin's parents die young or old? *Old*

7) Why did Franklin leave his brother's printing shop and Boston?
His brother beat him, and he wanted to start his own printing business.
Where did he finally go? *Philadelphia*

8) What offer does the Governor make to Franklin?
He offers to help him start a printing business in Philadelphia.

9) How did Franklin improve his writing skills?
By reading and then imitating "The Spectator" by Joseph Addison

BENJAMIN FRANKLIN
- THE AUTOBIOGRAPHY OF BENJAMIN FRANKLIN
WEEK 8

CRITICAL READING QUESTIONS (CONTINUED):

10) What did Franklin want to do with his life instead of what his father had chosen?
Go to sea

11) Why did Franklin become a vegetarian?
He read a book about it and realized it was cheaper, and he felt more alert and energetic as a result.

12) In improving his language, Franklin chose to take on what attitude or demeanor when arguing with others? *One of a humble inquirer and doubter*

Do you think this is a good idea? *Opinion*

13) What was Franklin's favorite book? *Pilgrim's Progress*

14) What did the old woman feed Franklin for dinner when he got off his boat from his journey? *Ox cheek*

15) What did Franklin look like when he first saw his future wife?
He had a loaf of bread under each arm and was eating one loaf.

16) What did the Governor say Franklin should be recommended to his father for?
Starting his own printing business

17) Does Franklin's diction reflect a quote he made: "Nothing should be expressed in two words that can be expressed in one"? Comment on his diction.
No, he uses complicated words and language and very long sentences.

BENJAMIN FRANKLIN
- The Autobiography of Benjamin Franklin

WEEK 8

MAKE IT REAL:

Find one quotation from *Poor Richard's Almanac*. (You will have to go online for this.)
Write it down, and memorize it.
Make sure you understand its meaning.

Examples:

"Success has ruined many a man."

"Necessity never made a good bargain."

"To lengthen thy life, lessen thy meals."

"Fish and visitors smell in three days."

BENJAMIN FRANKLIN
- THE AUTOBIOGRAPHY OF BENJAMIN FRANKLIN

WEEK 8

WRITING ASSIGNMENT:

You will be planning a persuasive essay this week much like Jonathan Edwards. (You will not write the actual essay yet.) Refer to *Write With The Best, Vol. 2* pages 92-93. Your topic will be "The Great Importance of an Education" or "Why You Must Receive an Excellent Education".

This week, you will write your thesis statement and your outline, and list specific examples of imagery, metaphors, and similes you will use to make your argument. You will use nature imagery similar to Edwards, and you can even borrow some of his examples.

After you plan your essay and write your thesis statement, write your outline. You can write a topical or sentence outline. Refer to pages 87-90 in *Write With the Best, Vol.2.*

BENJAMIN FRANKLIN
- *THE AUTOBIOGRAPHY OF BENJAMIN FRANKLIN*

WEEK 8

CULMINATING ACTIVITY:

Create a brief 5 minute news clip or radio broadcast called "Hero of the Week" outlining Franklin's life so far. Use the same diction Franklin used.

Benjamin Franklin
– The Autobiography of Benjamin Franklin

Week 9

Benjamin Franklin

"Would you live with ease, do what you ought, not what you please."

Words To Know:

Identify the part of speech of each word, and give one or two synonyms for each.

remit	Verb	send, transfer, address, dispatch
vexation	Noun	irritation, agitation, annoyance
queries	Noun	demand for answers, concerns, doubts, inquiries
confuting	Verb	disproving, refuting, contradicting, confounding
ingenious	Adj.	clever, brilliant, intelligent, artistic, bright
genteel	Adj.	sophisticated, cultured, aristocratic, confined
conferred	Verb	discussed, deliberated, advised, consulted
eminent	Adj.	very important, famous, august, celebrated
candidly	Adv.	frankly, honestly, sincerely
facetious	Adj.	tongue-in-cheek, amusing, comical, clever
genteel	Adj.	sophisticatedly, aristocratically, etc.
abatement	Noun	lessening, decline, decrease, discount, reduction
jocular	Adj.	funny, playful, amusing, blithe, cheerful, crazy
expostulated	Verb	reasoned with, argued, dissuaded, opposed, protested
sagacious	Adj.	smart, judicious, acute, canny
intimation	Noun	clue, hint, allusion, implication, indication
compunction	Noun	regret, sorrow, contrition
traduce	Verb	violate, disagree, malign, slander

BENJAMIN FRANKLIN
- THE AUTOBIOGRAPHY OF BENJAMIN FRANKLIN
WEEK 9

LITERARY ANALYSIS:

Periodic sentence: A long sentence that does not give the main clause or full meaning until the end of the sentence.
Writers often use periodic sentences to produce suspense.
Periodic sentences were used extensively by many eighteenth-century writers.

Example: "*Looking as if she were being haunted by devils, ignoring all danger, the girl ran.*"

Syntax: The way words are put together to form phrases and sentences.
Syntax concerns sentence structure and how that structure represents the tone and attitude of the author.

CRITICAL READING QUESTIONS:

1) What did Franklin do for his friend Collins? *Paid his bills for him*

2) Did Collins repay his debt to Franklin? *No*

3) Who did Franklin think was one of the best men in the world? *The Governor*
Was he correct? *No*
What did he later discover about this person? *He did not keep his promises, and he was dishonest and did not write the letters of credit.*

4) Was Franklin able to see his own shortcomings and make correct judgments about them? *Yes*
Give an example. *He comments that his father was right when he said he was too young to manage an important business.*

5) What justification did Franklin give for his return to eating meat (fish)?
He said fish ate other fish, so it was okay for him to eat them.

6) What kind of friends did Franklin find after Collins?
Friends who loved to read and write; some were moral.

Read With the Best

BENJAMIN FRANKLIN
- The Autobiography of Benjamin Franklin

WEEK 9

CRITICAL READING QUESTIONS (CONTINUED):

7) What piece of Scripture did Franklin and his friends try to improve upon? *Psalm 18*

8) Why did Franklin's friendship with Ralph dissolve?
Franklin tried to become familiar with his girlfriend.

Did Ralph and Franklin show admirable character? *No*

9) What had happened to Ms. Read during Franklin's absence?
She had married someone else.

10) What warning does Samuel Mickle give Franklin? *He tells him not to start a printing company in Philadelphia because of the failing economy.*

11) What was the name of Franklin's club? *Junto Club*
When did they meet? *Friday nights*

12) What rule was made in the club to avoid arguments? *Opinions could not be stated as completely positive and true or negative and false.*

13) Why did Franklin become a Deist? *The arguments he read by Deists appeared to him to be much stronger than the ones against Deism.*

What is a Deist?
Deism is a system of thought that bases religion on human morality and reason rather than divine revelation from God. Most Deists believe that God is not concerned with the personal concerns of man or involved personally at all in the lives of His people.

BENJAMIN FRANKLIN
- THE AUTOBIOGRAPHY OF BENJAMIN FRANKLIN

WEEK 9

CRITICAL READING QUESTIONS (CONTINUED):

14) According to Franklin, what three character traits were of the utmost importance "to the felicity of life" when dealing with other men? *Truth, sincerity, and integrity*

15) Find an example of a periodic sentence that Franklin uses. How does Franklin's syntax affect the tone of his autobiography?
Answers will vary. There are several examples. (One example is in the last few sentences of the Autobiography.) Franklin's syntax is somewhat formal and at times complicated, and this gives the autobiography more of a serious tone.

MAKE IT REAL:

Find another quotation from *Poor Richard's Almanac*.
Write it down, and memorize it.
Make sure you understand its meaning.

_____

_____

_____

_____

_____

_____

_____

_____

_____

_____

Benjamin Franklin
- The Autobiography of Benjamin Franklin
Week 9

Writing Assignment:

This week you will write your persuasive essay entitled: "The Great Importance of an Education" or "Why You Must Receive an Excellent Education".
- Follow the guidelines in *Write With The Best, Vol. 2* pages 92-93.
- Your essay should be 5 paragraphs.
- Don't forget your thesis statement, your attention grabber in your introduction and your lasting thought or attention grabber in the conclusion.
- Use the proofreading checklist for a persuasive essay to proofread your writing.

BENJAMIN FRANKLIN
- THE AUTOBIOGRAPHY OF BENJAMIN FRANKLIN

WEEK 9

CULMINATING ACTIVITY:

Alone or in groups, create a periodic sentence about Franklin's autobiography. Present it orally.

BENJAMIN FRANKLIN
- The Autobiography of Benjamin Franklin

Week 10

BENJAMIN FRANKLIN

"Humility makes great men twice honorable."

Literary Analysis:

Style: The way a writer arranges words and uses syntax and diction to convey his ideas. Style involves the unique way the author expresses himself and includes the author's diction, syntax, and figurative language.

Aphorism: A brief saying intended to teach a truth or belief. Another word for aphorism is an adage, proverb, or maxim.

Words To Know:

Identify the part of speech of each word, and give one or two synonyms for each.

arduous	Adj.	difficult, hard to endure, burdensome, harsh, heavy, formidable, exhausting
expeditiously	Adv.	efficiently, in a state of clarity, rapidity, or speed, promptly
gratis	Adj.	free, complimentary, gratuitous
incorrigible	Adj.	bad, hopeless, abandoned, inveterate, incurable
indefatigable	Adj.	untiring, active, assiduous, determined, diligent, energetic
multifarious	Adj.	diverse, assorted, manifold, many, miscellaneous, multiple
rectitude	Noun	uprightness, goodness, honesty, integrity, morality, decency
sanguine	Adj.	happy, optimistic, animated, buoyant, cheerful, assured
augmented	Verb	made greater, improved, aggrandized, amplified
avarice	Noun	avidity, extreme greed, frugality, covetousness
conferred	Verb	discussed, deliberated, advised, argued, consulted
insolent	Adj.	bold, disrespectful, abusive, arrogant, brazen
harangue	Noun	long lecture, address, discourse, speech

Read With the Best

BENJAMIN FRANKLIN
- *THE AUTOBIOGRAPHY OF BENJAMIN FRANKLIN*

WEEK 10

WORDS TO KNOW (CONTINUED):

polemic	Noun	argumentative, art of debating, contentious
artifice	Noun	hoax, clever act, con, contrivance, device, gambit
benevolent	Adj.	charitable, kind, altruistic

Use 3 words to write a sentence about Franklin's list of virtues.

_____

_____

_____

_____

CRITICAL READING QUESTIONS:

1) Why do you think Franklin is called "The Father of the American Dream"?
He became successful after coming from poverty by working hard.

2) What is scarce in 1729? *Paper money*

3) What is Franklin's first public contribution?
The first public library in North America

4) Why does Franklin want to be "completely virtuous"?
To benefit himself, to achieve moral perfection and to have a good reputation;
He believes it will advance his personal goals.

5) What do the two letters that Franklin receives ask of him?
To finish his autobiography and then publish it

6) What goal does Franklin set for himself? *To reach moral perfection*

Read With the Best

BENJAMIN FRANKLIN
- THE AUTOBIOGRAPHY OF BENJAMIN FRANKLIN

WEEK 10

CRITICAL READING QUESTIONS (CONTINUED):

7) Who did Franklin think were the two best examples of humility?
Jesus and Socrates

8) How many virtues did Franklin try to attain? *12*

Which virtue did he add? *Humility*

Why? *Because his friend told him he was prideful*

9) How long did Franklin plan to develop each virtue?
A week for each, until each one was conquered

10) What did Franklin say was the best way to serve God? *By serving man first*

11) Which virtue gave Franklin the most trouble? *Order*

12) Name the three virtues you think are most important and tell why.
Opinion; answers will vary

BENJAMIN FRANKLIN
- THE AUTOBIOGRAPHY OF BENJAMIN FRANKLIN

WEEK 10

MAKE IT REAL:

Try to come up with your own aphorism such as Franklin wrote in *Poor Richard's Almanac*. Your aphorism should offer advice about living simply or the value of hard work and frugality.

_____

_____

_____

_____

_____

_____

_____

_____

_____

_____

_____

_____

_____

_____

_____

_____

_____

_____

Read With the Best

Benjamin Franklin
- The Autobiography of Benjamin Franklin
Week 10

Writing Assignment:

You will be learning how to write a book review this week. (You will only learn about it this week – you will not write it.) You will be writing a book review on Ben Franklin's autobiography.

This week, complete page 50 in *Write With The Best, Vol. 2*, Days 11-14 only.

BENJAMIN FRANKLIN
- *THE AUTOBIOGRAPHY OF BENJAMIN FRANKLIN*

WEEK 10

CULMINATING ACTIVITY:

In groups or alone, list Franklin's virtues that he felt procured the following for him:
- Long life
- Good health
- Wealth
- The respect of his countrymen

You may need to refer to his autobiography for Franklin's comments on these.

JOHN AND ABIGAIL ADAMS
- THE LETTERS OF JOHN AND ABIGAIL ADAMS

WEEK 11

JOHN ADAMS   ABIGAIL ADAMS

"A Constitution of Government once changed from Freedom, can never be restored. Liberty, once lost, is lost forever."

BACKGROUND CHECK:

1) What kind of education did Abigail receive as a child?
No formal schooling, but a lot of reading and learning

2) What was the first political office John Adams held?
Delegate of First Continental Congress
Which President was he? *2nd President*

3) How many years was John Adams a famous and controversial figure in American public life?
26 years

4) When were the letters between Abigail and John written?
Between 1774 and 1783 when John was in Paris and Philadelphia

How many letters were written? *Over 300 letters*

5) Why are the letters so significant for America?
They provide a portrait of our young nation and its independence.

John and Abigail Adams
- The Letters of John and Abigail Adams

WEEK 11

Literary Analysis:

Voice: The speaker's or narrator's view on a specific idea as expressed in a literary passage. Voice also involves how all the elements of style are used to express the speaker's feelings.

Words To Know:

Identify the part of speech of each word, and give one or two synonyms for each.

futurity	Noun	coming time, future, coming ages, afterlife
irresolute	Adj.	indecisive, changing, doubtful, faltering, fearful, fickle
confiscation	Noun	seizure, appropriation, abduction, catching, stealing, acquisition
caprice	Noun	sudden change in behavior, changeableness, fickleness, impulse, inconsistency
Discretion	Noun	caution, judgment, acumen, concern, care, attention
pernicious	Adj.	bad, hurtful, damaging, dangerous
overweening	Adj.	arrogant, brash, conceited, haughty
exorbitant	Adj.	extravagant, excessive, extreme, enormous, expensive
languid	Adj.	dropping, dull, comatose, listless
duped	Adj.	baffled, fooled, cheated, bamboozled, deceived
rue (verb)	Verb	regret, apologize, deplore, grieve, mourn
dissipate	Verb	expend, spend, consume, deplete
expunged	Verb	destroyed, obliterated, abolished, annihilated
induced	Verb	encouraged, caused to happen, actuated, brought about, caused, effected
cordial (noun)	Noun	a liquor drink, any invigorating or stimulating preparation
avocations	Noun	hobbies, amusements, diversions, pastimes
solicitude	Noun	worry, anxiety, attention, care, concern;
solicitous	Adj.	worried, anxious, apprehensive, ardent
portends	~~Noun~~ (NO)	omens, warnings, foreshadowings

Use 3 adjectives from this list to describe the relationship between John and Abigail Adams.

_____

_____

_____

_____

JOHN AND ABIGAIL ADAMS
- THE LETTERS OF JOHN AND ABIGAIL ADAMS

WEEK 11

CRITICAL READING QUESTIONS:

1) What can you tell about Abigail's level of intelligence and education from her first letter?
She was very well read and educated in history, etc. and used many historical references.

2) Name three allusions Abigail uses in her letters.
Julius Caesar – the Ides of March; Philip of Macedon; Sparta invaded by Philip; Rome not built in a day – Polibius; Other various answers also

3) What was the "Frown of Providence" among the troops? *Small pox*

What type of figurative language is this? *Metaphor*

4) What can you infer about the relationship between Abigail and John from their letters?
Answers may vary but should include: They were the dearest of friends and lovers. They were united in a common cause. They were intellectual partners or peers.

5) Find an example of parallelism in the letters.
Answers will vary, but two good examples are: "to ripen their judgments, dissipate their fears, allure their hopes"; "choose officers, make laws, and mend roads"

6) According to John Adams, how should the 2nd of July be looked at for future generations?
As deliverance from God and it should be celebrated extensively by solemn acts of devotion to God

Read With the Best | Diagnostic Prescriptive Services | www.edudps.com

JOHN AND ABIGAIL ADAMS
- The Letters of John and Abigail Adams

WEEK 11

CRITICAL READING QUESTIONS (CONTINUED):

7) What does Abigail compare John's expressions of tenderness to?
Cordial (medicinal drink)

What type of figurative language is this? *A metaphor*

8) What did John omit in his letter that was essential to Abigail's happiness?
Words about his health, himself, or his situation

9) If these letters were not labeled, how could you differentiate Abigail's voice from John's? Name some differences in the two voices.
John's letters are more organized, formal, and political; whereas, Abigail's are more personal and somewhat scattered and tender; Abigail used more poetical phrases, but John did not use as many.

MAKE IT REAL:

List 2-3 differences in the way we would write a personal letter today from the way these letters were written. What is lost in our writing today? Is this good or bad?
Answers will vary, but should include some mention of the verbal skill, formality, and figurative language used by Abigail and John Adams.

_____
_____
_____
_____
_____
_____

Read With the Best

JOHN AND ABIGAIL ADAMS
- The Letters of John and Abigail Adams

WEEK 11

WRITING ASSIGNMENT:

This week you will write your book review on Benjamin Franklin's autobiography. Complete Days 15-20 in *Write With the Best, Vol. 2 on pages 54-56.*

JOHN AND ABIGAIL ADAMS
- The Letters of John and Abigail Adams

WEEK 11

CULMINATING ACTIVITY:

As a group activity or alone, take one of the Adams' letters and paraphrase it in modern language. Present it to an audience.

THOMAS PAINE
- *COMMON SENSE / THE CRISIS*, NO. 1

WEEK 12

> *"These are the times that try men's souls. The summer soldier and the sunshine patriot will, in this crisis, shrink from the service of their country; but he that stands it now, deserves the love and thanks of men and women."*

THOMAS PAINE

BACKGROUND CHECK:

1) How was Paine like Benjamin Franklin?
Self taught, curious about everything, successful from a poor background, a Deist, lover of the sea

2) Was Paine a Christian? *No*

3) Why did Paine write his pamphlets anonymously?
They were against England, and he would be charged with treason.

4) How many copies of *Common Sense* were sold? *Half a million copies*

5) Why did Paine not last in public employment or political appointments?
He was too hot tempered and indiscreet.

6) How popular were his two books in 18th century America? *Very popular*

7) To what army was *The Crisis* read out loud? *Washington's army*

Thomas Paine
— *Common Sense / The Crisis*, No. 1
Week 12

WORDS TO KNOW:

Identify the part of speech of each word, and give one or two synonyms for each.

relinquish	Verb	give up, let go, abandon, desert
procure	Verb	acquire, obtain, annex, appropriate, corral
superseded (superceded)	Verb	took the place of, overrode, abandoned, annulled, displaced
fallacious	Adj.	false, wrong, deceptive, incorrect, invalid, illogical, irrational, out of date
reproach	Verb or Noun	find fault with, admonish, criticize, condemn; strong criticism, dishonor, abuse, blame
gratuitous	Adj.	free, complimentary, chargeless, spontaneous, voluntary
farcical	Adj.	absurd, amusing, comical, droll, funny, nonsensical
espouse	Verb	stand up for, support, accept, approve, advocate, defend
precariousness	Noun	instability, anxiety, changeability, disquiet, inconsistency
repugnant	Adj.	bad, obnoxious, hostile, abhorrent, abominable
extirpated	Verb	destroyed, uprooted, abated, abolished, annihilated
impious	Adj.	not religious, agnostic, immoral, irreverent, apostate
ague	Noun	shivering, fear, chills, fever
apparition	Noun	ghost, chimera, delusion, hallucination, haunt, illusion, phantasm
penitentially	Adv.	remorsefully, apologetically, contritely, regretfully, mournfully
servile	Adj.	groveling, subservient, abject, base, humbling
ardor	Noun	enthusiasm, avidity, devotion, eagerness, fervor
sottish	Adj.	alcoholic, drunken, boozy
complicit	Adj.	guilt in crime or offense, associated with or participating in an activity, especially one of questioning nature
sycophant	Noun	person who caters to another, fan, minion, puppet, slave, parasite

Read With the Best

THOMAS PAINE
- COMMON SENSE / THE CRISIS, NO. 1

WEEK 12

LITERARY ANALYSIS:

Alliteration: The repetition of consonant sounds (usually initial consonant sounds) to make a point.

Example: "She sells seashells by the seashore."

CRITICAL READING QUESTIONS:

1) In the introduction of *Common Sense,* Paine says he has purposely avoided what?
Personal concerns and personal details

2) Paine contends that the cause of America is the cause of whom?
All mankind

3) Why does Paine say his book is called *Common Sense*?
Paine contends that what he is saying contains the simple facts and plain, common sense.

4) In *Common Sense,* what types of people does Paine say might seek reconciliation with Britain?
Weak, prejudiced men who cannot be trusted and who think better of Europe than they should

5) Paine says it is against *nature* to reconcile with Great Britain.

6) List three specific brutalities of the British listed in *Common Sense.*
Causing poverty, destroying personal property, murdering civilians, inflicting starvation, taxing the people, and more

7) What kind of person is "the summer soldier and the sunshine patriot"?
Someone who supports a cause only when it is convenient, safe, or to his advantage

THOMAS PAINE
– *COMMON SENSE / THE CRISIS*, NO. 1
WEEK 12

CRITICAL READING QUESTIONS (CONTINUED):

8) How does Paine establish his tone in the first paragraph of *The Crisis*?

He uses harsh words to describe British domination – "hell" and "slavery."

What is his tone?

His tone is emotional, fervent, enthusiastic and could be called harsh and somber; it can also be called foreboding.

9) Give the examples of alliteration in the opening lines of *The Crisis*. How does alliteration make you remember this famous line?

These are the "times that try men's souls", "The summer soldier and the sunshine patriot will shrink from the service"; alliteration is easier to memorize.

10) What is Paine's purpose in writing *The Crisis*?

To encourage the soldiers to continue their fight and to tell them it was well worth it

11) What does Paine compare the struggle for freedom to in the last paragraphs?

The invasion of one's home by a murderous robber. He says anyone would defend this.

12) In both of Paine's passages, what device does he use that serves as a good attention grabber?

Alliteration

THOMAS PAINE
COMMON SENSE / THE CRISIS, No. 1

WEEK 12

MAKE IT REAL:

Find at least 3 questions used by Paine in his two works. What is the effect of these questions?
Examples can include:
"Has your house been burned?"
"Has your house been destroyed before your face?"
"Can you restore to us the time that has passed?"
These questions are intended to cause thinking and action in the readers.

THOMAS PAINE
- COMMON SENSE / THE CRISIS, NO. 1

WEEK 12

WRITING ASSIGNMENT:

You will begin to learn how to write and deliver a persuasive speech this week. Complete pages 64-68, Days 1-4 only in *Write With The Best, Vol. 2.* You will not actually write your speech this week. Topics will be given next week.

Thomas Paine
Common Sense / The Crisis, No. 1

WEEK 12

CULMINATING ACTIVITY:

Alone or in groups, find at least 3 aphorisms that Paine writes in both *Common Sense* and *The Crisis*.
Why are these considered aphorisms?
Answers may vary, but examples are:
"What we obtain too cheap, we esteem too lightly."
"Tyranny, like hell, is not easily conquered."
These are witty and pithy sayings that are easy to remember.

PATRICK HENRY - Speech in the Virginia Convention
THOMAS JEFFERSON - From *The Autobiography of Thomas Jefferson* and "The Declaration of Independence"

WEEK 13

> *"I know not what course others may take; but as for me, give me liberty or give me death!"*

PATRICK HENRY

BACKGROUND CHECK:

Note: You will have to do some research on your own to answer these questions.

1) Were Patrick Henry's speeches written down when he spoke them?
No, they were pieced together years after his death.

2) What were two of Henry's occupations?
Farmer, lawyer, Virginia House of Burgesses, Governor of Virginia

3) What two things is Henry most known for?
Writing and delivering two best-known speeches of the Revolution and leading the movement to add the Bill of Rights to the Constitution

PATRICK HENRY - Speech in the Virginia Convention
THOMAS JEFFERSON - From *The Autobiography of Thomas Jefferson* and "The Declaration of Independence"

WEEK 13

PATRICK HENRY
WORDS TO KNOW:

Identify the part of speech of each word, and give one or two synonyms for each.

arduous	Adj.	difficult, hard to endure, burdensome, formidable, grueling
avert	Verb	thwart, avoid by turning away, avoid, deflect, deter, divert
comport	Verb	agree, accord, check, conform
delusive	Adj.	deceptive, apparent, chimerical, fallacious, false, illusive
extenuate	Verb	lessen, mitigate, decrease, diminish, downplay
insidious	Adj.	sneaky, tricky, artful, astute, corrupt, crafty, cunning
prostrate	Adj.	flat, horizontal, abject, prone, helpless, beaten, defenseless, impotent
remonstrate	Verb	argue against, blame, censure, challenge, combat, complain, criticize
magnitude	Noun	importance, consequence, degree, imminence, grandeur, greatness, size, amount, breadth, bulk
formidable	Adj.	horrible, terrifying, appalling, awful, dangerous
subjugation	Noun	bondage, slavery, servitude, subjection
irresolution	Noun	hesitation, delay, doubt, fluctuation, reluctance

LITERARY ANALYSIS:

Rhetoric: The art of using words to persuade.

Rhetorical Question: A question in persuasive writing used to produce an effect or make a statement, but not expected to be answered. A rhetorical question makes a bigger impression on a reader than a regular statement.

PATRICK HENRY - Speech in the Virginia Convention
THOMAS JEFFERSON - From *The Autobiography of Thomas Jefferson* and "The Declaration of Independence"

WEEK 13

PATRICK HENRY
CRITICAL READING QUESTIONS:

1) Who does Henry "revere above all earthly kings"?

God

2) Find three examples of figurative language that Henry uses to persuade his listeners.

"Lamp of experience," "Our chains are forged," "The storm coming on," "Delusive phantom of hope"

3) Give two Biblical allusions used by Henry.

"those who having eyes see not," "suffer not yourselves to be betrayed with a kiss"

4) Because Henry was such a great orator, he frequently used rhetorical questions and repetition to make his point. Find an example of each.

There are several examples, but some may include: "And what have we to oppose to them? Shall we try argument?"

He repeats the words "Sir", "Mr. President," "let it come!"

5) Find one example of parallelism used by Henry.

"We have petitioned, we have remonstrated, we have supplicated, we have prostrated."

PATRICK HENRY - Speech in the Virginia Convention
THOMAS JEFFERSON - From *The Autobiography of Thomas Jefferson* and "The Declaration of Independence"

WEEK 13

> *"We hold these truths to be self-evident, that all men are created equal, that they are endowed by their Creator with certain unalienable Rights, that among these are Life, Liberty and the pursuit of Happiness."*

THOMAS JEFFERSON

BACKGROUND CHECK:

1) On what day did Thomas Jefferson die?

July 4

Who else died the same day?

John Adams

2) What was Jefferson's first occupation?

Lawyer

Name four other interests or occupations he had in his lifetime.

Violinist, horseman, statesmen, President, author, collector of books, art patron

3) What kind of family did he come from?

Wealthy and distinguished

4) What is Jefferson most famous for?

Being the author of "The Declaration of Independence"

PATRICK HENRY - Speech in the Virginia Convention
THOMAS JEFFERSON - From *The Autobiography of Thomas Jefferson* and "The Declaration of Independence"

WEEK 13

THOMAS JEFFERSON
WORDS TO KNOW:

Identify the part of speech of each word, and give one or two synonyms for each.

abdicate	Verb	give up a right, position, or power, abandon, abjure, leave, drop, forgo
allurement	Noun	lure, bait, inducement, invitation, attraction, allure, appeal, draw, charm
annihilation	Noun	utter destruction, demolition, massacre, slaughter, ruin
complaisance	Noun	agreeableness, acquiesce, compliance, courtesy, friendliness, kindliness
obtrude	Verb	thrust outward, impose, infringe, interfere, intrude
opprobrium	Noun	disgrace, blemish, degradation, discredit, humiliation, disrespect
pusillanimous	Adj.	fearful, afraid, cowardly, tame, timid, anxious, apprehensive
redress	Noun	help, compensation, aid, amendment, assistance, atonement
unremitting	Adj.	continual, connected, consecutive, constant, endless, enduring
usurpation	Noun	seizing something, apprehension, appropriation, arrest, assumption
transient	Adj.	temporary, brief, changeable, ephemeral, evanescent, fleeting, flash

Use 4 words from Henry's and Jefferson's vocabulary to write a sentence about both of their writings.
Answers will vary.

_____

_____

_____

_____

PATRICK HENRY - Speech in the Virginia Convention
THOMAS JEFFERSON - From *The Autobiography of Thomas Jefferson* and "The Declaration of Independence"

Week 13

THOMAS JEFFERSON
CRITICAL READING QUESTIONS:

1) In the second paragraph of "The Declaration", who does Jefferson blame for the wrongs done to the American colonies?
King George III

2) What three parts does Jefferson include in "The Declaration" that are included in every good persuasive speech or essay?
Introduction, Body, Conclusion

3) Who was the last colony to approve "The Declaration"?
New York

4) What literary device does Jefferson use to list the offenses of King George?
Parallelism or parallel structure

5) How does Jefferson say the king has answered the repeated petitions of the colonists?
With repeated inquiries

6) How many years does Jefferson say the king has been a "tyrant" over them?
12 years

7) Who does Jefferson say the writers of "The Declaration" appeal to for "the rectitude of their intentions"?
"The supreme judge of the world": God

8) What two parts did Jefferson say were left out of the final draft?
Censures on the people of England as a whole and disagreement with slavery

PATRICK HENRY - Speech in the Virginia Convention
THOMAS JEFFERSON - From *The Autobiography of Thomas Jefferson* and "The Declaration of Independence"

MAKE IT REAL:

Find one famous quote from Henry's or Jefferson's writing, and memorize it. Be prepared to quote it orally.

PATRICK HENRY - Speech in the Virginia Convention
THOMAS JEFFERSON - From *The Autobiography of Thomas Jefferson* and "The Declaration of Independence"

WEEK 13

WRITING ASSIGNMENT:

This week you will write your outline and introduction only for your persuasive speech on a topic from the list at the bottom of the page.
Complete pages 68-69 and Days 5-6 only in *Write With The Best, Vol. 2*.
Next week you will finish writing your speech and prepare to deliver it to an audience.

Choose from one of these topics:
- Abortion
- Infanticide
- Euthanasia
- Immorality in America
- The Takeover of Technology and Technological Devices in our Society
- Why The Church Needs A True Revival
- Why Our Educational System Needs Reform
- Why The Driving Age For Teenagers Should Remain Sixteen

Also remember to use the same persuasive techniques you use in a persuasive essay.

_____
_____
_____
_____
_____
_____
_____
_____
_____
_____

PATRICK HENRY - Speech in the Virginia Convention
THOMAS JEFFERSON - From *The Autobiography of Thomas Jefferson* and "The Declaration of Independence"

CULMINATING ACTIVITY:

Alone or as a group, create a T.V. commercial trying to sell and promote either Henry's speech or "The Declaration of Independence." You must emphasize the most important parts of each.

PHILLIS WHEATLY -
"On Being Brought from Africa to America"
"On the Death of Rev. Mr. George Whitfield, 1770"
"To His Excellency General Washington"

WEEK 14

PHILLIS WHEATLY

*"Remember, Christians,
Negroes, black as Cain,
May be refined,
and join the angelic train."*

BACKGROUND CHECK:

1) How did Wheatly get her first and last name?

Last name from her slave owner and first name from the ship that carried her to America

2) Which English poets influenced her?

Milton, Pope, Gray

3) What poem made her famous?

"On the Death of the Rev. Mr. George Whitefield"

4) When and by whom was Wheatly's poetry rediscovered and appreciated?

1830's by New England abolitionists

5) What two traditions did Wheatly start in America?

The Black American Literary Tradition and the Black Woman's Literary tradition

Phillis Wheatly -
"On Being Brought from Africa to America"
"On the Death of Rev. Mr. George Whitfield, 1770"
"To His Excellency General Washington"

WEEK 14

Words To Know:

Identify the part of speech of each word, and give one or two synonyms for each.

diabolic	Adj.	evil, fiendish, atrocious, cruel, demonic
benighted	Adj.	unenlightened, dark, ignorant, primitive, simple
sable	Adj.	very dark in color, black, dark, ebony, gloomy, murky, somber
wonted	Adj.	usual, accustomed, common, conventional, customary, familiar
deplore	Verb	regret, condemn, abhor, bemoan, carry on, censure
incessant	Adj.	never-ending, persistent, constant, continual, continuous, endless
reaminates	Verb	refresh, recruit, comfort, make feel better, revive, regenerate, rejuvenate
refulgent	Adj.	glowing, bright, brilliant, luminous, radiant, resplendent, shining
bemoan	Verb	express sorrow, complain, regret, deplore, rue, mourn, lament
propitious	Adj.	full of promise, good, favorable, advantageous, auspicious, beneficial, encouraging, bright, fortunate
refluent	Adj.	flowing back, ebbing
array	Noun	collection, considerable group, arrangement, body, bunch, bundle, cluster, design, display, disposition
pensive	Adj.	meditative, solemn, absorbed, attentive, contemplative, dreamy, musing
ensign	Noun	flag, colors, emblem, standard, symbol

Literary Analysis:

Theme: The central and dominating idea in a literary work.

Symbol: An object, image, feeling, color, place, or event that represents an idea or stands for something else.

Examples: The cross represents Christianity.
The flag stands for patriotism.

PHILLIS WHEATLY -
"On Being Brought from Africa to America"
"On the Death of Rev. Mr. George Whitfield, 1770"
"To His Excellency General Washington"

WEEK 14

CRITICAL READING QUESTIONS:

1) In "On Being Brought from Africa", what metaphor does Wheatly use to describe the way many people view black people?
"Their colour is a diabolic dye".

2) What verse form is this poem written in?
Heroic couplets

3) What might the words "benighted soul", "sable race", and "diabolic dye" symbolize about "unreceptive man"?
That these men are in spiritual darkness/ blackness

4) What evidence does Wheatly use to prove that Africans can also become Christians?
Her conversion to Christianity

5) Who is this poem addressed to?
Christians

6) Who is Wheatly talking to in the first stanza of "On the Death of George Whitefield"?
George Whitefield

7) In stanza one, who is "the setting sun"? What type of figurative language is this?
George Whitefield, metaphor

8) In stanza three, Wheatly gives an example of Whitefield's what?
Sermons/ discourses

PHILLIS WHEATLY -
"On Being Brought from Africa to America"
"On the Death of Rev. Mr. George Whitfield, 1770"
"To His Excellency General Washington"

WEEK 14

CRITICAL READING QUESTIONS (CONTINUED):

9) What does Wheatly tell us in stanza one about Whitefield's oratory or speaking skills?
His sermons were unequaled and eloquent and like music; they inflamed the heart and captivated the mind.

10) In "To His Excellency General Washington", which phrases portray America as divine or divinely guided?
"heaven- defended race", "see the bright beams of heaven's revolving light", "she moves divinely fair"

11) Who is the "goddess" and "Columbia"? *America*
What type of figurative language is this? *personification*

12) What are Great Britain's actions and feelings toward Columbia?
They are blind to America's needs and suffering and only want power.

13) What is the general theme of this poem?
May God guide George Washington as he leads America in her divine purpose/ America is called by God and Washington will lead her/ God's Sovereignty over America

Read With the Best — Diagnostic Prescriptive Services | www.edudps.com

Phillis Wheatly -
"On Being Brought from Africa to America"
"On the Death of Rev. Mr. George Whitfield, 1770"
"To His Excellency General Washington"

Week 14

Make It Real:

Think of three symbols in our society today, in the past societies, or in literature. *__Answers will vary. Examples can be: The American flag for our nation, the swastika for Nazi Germany, a rose for youth and beauty, etc.__*

Phillis Wheatly -
"On Being Brought from Africa to America"
" On the Death of Rev. Mr. George Whitfield, 1770"
" To His Excellency General Washington"

WEEK 14

Writing Assignment:

This week, you will complete your persuasive speech you started last week.
Write the body of your speech and conclusion and practice reading your speech out loud. Refer to Days 8-10 on pages 69-71 in *Write With the Best, Vol. 2.*
Use the checklist on page 112.
Proofread your speech.
Make sure you include rhetorical questions and persuasive techniques in your speech.

Culminating Activity:

Alone or in groups, read and paraphrase each stanza of Wheatly's poem "Thoughts on Works of Providence"in one sentence paraphrases.

_____

_____

_____

_____

_____

_____

_____

_____

_____

_____

_____

Washington Irving
- "Rip Van Winkle"

WEEK 15

WASHINGTON IRVING

"A tart temper never mellows with age; and a sharp tongue is the only edged tool that grows keener with constant use."

BACKGROUND CHECK:

1) Name two unique facts about Irving related to American literature.
He was the first American writer to achieve an international literary reputation, one of the inventors of the modern short story, and the first American to support himself solely through his writing.

2) Which book of Irving's made him famous?
The Sketch Book

3) What two famous writers were inspired by *The Sketchbook* as young school boys?
Hawthorne and Longfellow

4) What is the name of the other famous short story, aside from "Rip Van Winkle," that Irving wrote?
"The Legend of Sleepy Hollow"

Washington Irving
- "Rip Van Winkle"

Week 15

Words To Know:

Identify the part of speech of each word, and give one or two synonyms for each.

scrupulous	Adj.	extremely careful, conscientious, critical, exact
deference	Noun	obedience, compliance, acquiesce, submission
decried	Verb	discovered, beheld, detected, discerned
martial	Adj.	having to do with armed hostilities, aggressive, bellicose, belligerent
obsequious	Adj.	groveling, submissive, abject, complacent, compliant
conciliating	Verb	placating, appeasing, pacifying, allaying, alleviating
termagant	Adj.	disorderly, disruptive, noisy, fractious, rowdy
malleable	Adj.	pliable, adaptable, compliant, flexible
insuperable	Adj.	impassable, impossible, insurmountable, overwhelming
assiduity	Noun	diligence, attention, care, concentration, effort
patrimonial	Adj.	ancestral, affiliated, congenital, inherited, familial
rubicund	Adj.	flushed, florid, healthy, rosy
keener	Adj.	ore enthusiastic, more animated, more anxious, more alert, more sharp, more piercing
sagely	Adv.	prudently, wisely, carefully, sensibly
approbation	Noun	praise, admiration, approval, consent
wistfully	Adv.	Lingingly, daydreaming, sadly, unhappily, sorrowfully, dismally
alacrity	Noun	liveliness, promptness, avidity, eagerness, enthusiasm
azure	Adj. Noun	purplish blue, sky, sea color, place where God lives, wonderful feeling, bliss
uncouth	Adj.	clumsy, uncultivated, awkward, barbaric, coarse, boorish
quaffed	Verb	drunk down, gulped, downed, swallowed
invariably	Adv.	perpetually, always, constantly, regularly
populous	Adj.	crowded, packed with inhabitants, dense, many, multifarious, busy, congested
connubial	Adj.	marital, married, matrimonial, concerning marriage
metamorphosed	Verb	converted, transformed, aged, altered, changed, developed
disputatious	Adj.	argumentative, cantankerous, captious, contentious
phlegm	Noun	apathy, disregard, indifference, aloofness
bilious	Adj.	peaked, pale, sick, ailing, ill, sickly, anxious, concerned, restless
harangue	Noun	long lecture, address, diatribe, speech, discourse
corroborated	Verb	approved, certified, checked out, confirmed, proved, justified, affirmed, vouched for
impunity	Noun	freedom, exception, exemption, liberty, privilege
torpor	Noun	lethargy, apathy, sloth, slumber, stupor, laziness
despotism	Noun	absolute power, tyranny, autocracy, dictatorship
venerable	Adj.	respected, admirable, aged, august, dignified, experienced, grand

Washington Irving
- "Rip Van Winkle"

Week 15

Words To Know (continued):

Use four of the "Words to Know" to describe the character of Rip Van Winkle.
Answers will vary.

_____

_____

_____

_____

_____

_____

_____

Literary Analysis:

Satire: A literary technique that blends humor with the ridicule of the faults, weaknesses, and stupidity of mankind.

Stereotype or Stock Character: A familiar character who appears so often in writing that he is immediately recognized. Some examples are the absent-minded professor or villain, etc.

Round Character: In the characterization of a story, the character who is fully developed, is complex, and stands out from all other characters as purely individual. The round character is portrayed in such a way that he is looked at as a real person.

Romanticism: A literary movement of the early 19th century that emphasized imagination and emotion over reason, mystery and the supernatural over common sense, and the supremacy of the individual over tradition and social convention.

Transcendentalism: A religious and literary movement that took place in the early 1800's and emphasized the importance of the individual conscience, intuition, and God's moral law that is revealed in nature.
Emerson and Thoreau are the main authors who revealed this philosophy.

WASHINGTON IRVING
- "Rip Van Winkle"

WEEK 15

CRITICAL READING QUESTIONS:

1) What is the setting (time and place) of this story ?
Colonial New York in the Catskill Mountains during the time of the reign of King George III and then after the Revolutionary War is over

2) Why might a "termagant" wife be considered a blessing?
She can teach the virtues of patience and long suffering to her husband.

3) Was Rip entirely lazy? *No*

4) Who was Rip's companion in idleness? *His dog Wolf*

5) What is the only edge tool that grows sharper by constant use? What type of literary term is this? *A sharp tongue; metaphor*

6) What sound initiates Rip's adventure into the Wilderness?
Someone calling his name

7) How long does Rip sleep? *20 years*

8) Who is the first one to recognize him when he returns? *An old neighbor woman*

9) What are some ways that Irving portrays Rip as a round character?
He makes his appearance and character traits unforgettable and makes Rip a realistic character by describing his idleness, his family, his reaction to his wife, etc.

10) What was "petticoat government"? *Being ruled by a woman/wife in a marriage*

WASHINGTON IRVING
- "Rip Van Winkle"

WEEK 15

CRITICAL READING QUESTIONS (CONTINUED):

11) What traits of Romanticism do you find in "Rip Van Winkle?"
Individualism found in Rip who follows his feelings rather than reason and a focus on nature and the mysterious

12) What is a major theme of "Rip Van Winkle"? ***Change, immutability***

13) In what ways is this a story of satire?
It parodies the sin of sloth and satirizes government and politics.

MAKE IT REAL:

Name at least one stereotype or stock character that Irving portrays in "Rip Van Winkle."
Answers will vary but can include: Rip Van Winkle's wife – a nag; Rip Van Winkle – a lazy, unproductive husband.

Washington Irving
- "Rip Van Winkle"

Week 15

WRITING ASSIGNMENT:

You will begin to learn to write a literary critique this week with a focus on the themes and Romanticism found in "Rip Van Winkle" you read this week and "The Last of the Mohicans" you will read next week.
Complete *Write With the Best, Vol. 2*, Days 1-4 only, pages 43-47.

WASHINGTON IRVING
- "Rip Van Winkle"

WEEK 15

CULMINATING ACTIVITY:

Alone or in a group, discuss the tone of "Rip Van Winkle." Find three examples of ways that Irving portrays the tone of this story. What literary devices does he use to portray this tone?

Answers will vary.

JAMES FENIMORE COOPER - FROM *THE LAST OF THE MOHICANS*
WILLIAM CULLEN BRYANT-"THANATOPSIS" & "TO A WATERFOWL"

WEEK 16

"Your fathers came from the setting sun, crossed the big river, fought the people of the country and took the land."

JAMES FENIMORE COOPER

BACKGROUND CHECK:

1) Who was one of the most popular characters in world literature?

<u>Natty Bumppo or Hawkeye</u>

2) What series is Cooper best known for? What part of Natty Bumppo's life does Cooper cover in this series?

<u>The Leatherstocking Tales</u> *or Series; from his youth to his death*

3) What books most influence Twain's *Huckleberry Finn*?

<u>The Leatherstocking Tales</u>

4) Were the *Leatherstocking Tales* well-read during their time?

<u>Yes</u>

JAMES FENIMORE COOPER – FROM *THE LAST OF THE MOHICANS*
WILLIAM CULLEN BRYANT – "THANATOPSIS" & "TO A WATERFOWL"

WEEK 16

JAMES FENIMORE COOPER

WORDS TO KNOW:

Identify the part of speech of each word, and give one or two synonyms for each.

sultriness	Noun	mugginess, dampness, humidity, humidness, oppressiveness
discordant	Adj.	not in harmony, conflicting, antagonistic, contradictory
accoutrements	Noun	clothing, apparel, gear, effects, equipment, apparatus, belongings
parentage	Noun	heritage, ancestry, antecedent, birth, blood, descent, family
attenuated	Verb	weakened, abated, contracted, crippled, dissipated, amalgamated
indurated	Verb	hardened, acclimated, amalgamated, calloused, buttressed, compacted, braced
guile	Noun	slyness, cleverness, artifice, chicanery, craft, cunning, deceit
disdain	Noun	hate, indifference, arrogance, antipathy, aversion, contempt, derision, despite
loth	Adj.	hostile, angry, loathsome, unpleasant, unwilling, reluctant
nettled	Verb	provoked, upset, annoyed, chafed, disgusted, disturbed, exasperated
guttural	Adj.	deep in sound, harsh, rough, thick, low

LITERARY ANALYSIS:

Apostrophe: A figure of speech in which an absent or dead person, an abstract quality, or something nonhuman is directly addressed.

Blank Verse: Verse written in unrhymed iambic pentameter (lines of 10 syllables each – odd numbered syllables are unaccented, even numbered syllables are accented). Blank verse does not rhyme, but does have a regular rhythm.

Elegy: A type of poem that meditates on death or mortality in a thoughtful way.

JAMES FENIMORE COOPER - FROM *THE LAST OF THE MOHICANS*
WILLIAM CULLEN BRYANT-"THANATOPSIS" & "TO A WATERFOWL"

WEEK 16

JAMES FENIMORE COOPER

CRITICAL READING QUESTIONS:

1) What was the setting of *The Last of the Mohicans*?
The French and Indian War in the wilderness of New York

2) What specific point of view does the author use to tell this story?
Third Person/ Objective (perhaps omniscient)

3) What kind of imagery does the author use to introduce this chapter? What senses does this imagery appeal to? *Imagery of nature; hearing, sight, touch*

4) What aspect of his characters does Cooper describe to reveal facts about their lives in paragraphs 3 and 4? *Their bodies and physical appearances*

5) What is Natty's Indian name? *Hawkeye*

6) What elements of Romanticism do you see in this story?
A respect and honor of nature, communion with nature, individualism, emotion

7) Why does Hawkeye not shoot the deer with a gun at the end of the story?
He doesn't want to make noise and show the enemy where they are.

8) What similar theme found in "Rip Van Winkle" do you find in Cooper's story?
Change and progress, preservation of tradition, change from war

9) Why do you think this book was called *The Last of the Mohicans*?
It was about the dying out of the Mohican Indian tribe because of the changes brought on by the white man.

Read With the Best

JAMES FENIMORE COOPER - FROM *THE LAST OF THE MOHICANS*
WILLIAM CULLEN BRYANT - "THANATOPSIS" & "TO A WATERFOWL"

"He, who from zone to zone, Guides through the boundless sky thy certain flight, in the long way that I must tread alone, will lead my steps aright."

WILLIAM CULLEN BRYANT

BACKGROUND CHECK:

1) Why was Bryant overlooked as a poet in his life time?
He refused to promote himself.

2) Which poem established his reputation?
"Thanatopsis"

3) Name two of Bryant's professions besides a poet.
Lawyer, judge, newspaper reporter, newspaper editor and owner, translator

James Fenimore Cooper - from *The Last of the Mohicans*
William Cullen Bryant - "Thanatopsis" & "To A Waterfowl"

WEEK 16

William Cullen Bryant

Words To Know:

Identify the part of speech of each word, and give one or two synonyms for each.

venerable	Adj.	respected, admirable, dignified, honorable, experienced, grand, elderly
musings	Noun	absorptions, contemplations, deliberations, meditations, reflections, thoughts
blight	Noun	disease, plague, affliction, bane, contamination, corruption
swain	Noun	beau, admirer, beloved, cavalier, escort, lover, suitor, sweetheart, admirer
hoary	Adj.	ancient, aged, antique, elderly, old, relic
mirth	Noun	great joy, amusement, entertainment, frolic, fun, glee, happiness
chafed	Verb	rubbed, grinded against, abraded, barked, damaged, eroded, irritated
illimitable	Adj.	endless, boundless, constant, continual, countless, enduring, everlasting
abyss	Noun	something very deep, usually a feature of land, chasm, depth, gorge, hole, pit

JAMES FENIMORE COOPER - FROM *THE LAST OF THE MOHICANS*
WILLIAM CULLEN BRYANT - "THANATOPSIS" & "TO A WATERFOWL"

WEEK 16

WILLIAM CULLEN BRYANT
CRITICAL READING QUESTIONS:

1) Name two things that are personified in "Thanatopsis." *Nature, Earth, Death, Ocean*

2) Why do you think Bryant wrote this poem in blank verse instead of rhyme?
The poem is an elegy; it sounds like the poet is speaking directly to the reader; it also makes the tone more serious.

3) What Transcendental philosophy does Bryant convey about man, death, and nature in "Thanatopsis"?
Man will become one with nature when he dies.

4) In lines 31-72, what terms are used to describe death?
Couches, lying down, slumber, last sleep, making one's bed, retire, tomb of man, departure

5) This entire poem concerns itself with what? Why is this poem called an elegy?
Contemplating or thinking about death; it is a meditation about death.

6) What is the rhyme scheme of "To A Waterfowl"? *Abab*

7) What apostrophe is found in the opening lines of "To A Waterfowl"?
Bryant is speaking to a waterfowl.

8) What does "the long way that I must tread alone" symbolize? *Life's journey*

9) How does rhyming verse better portray the tone of this poem?
The tone is more hopeful, and rhyme seems better suited for this tone and conveys more emotion.

JAMES FENIMORE COOPER - FROM *THE LAST OF THE MOHICANS*
WILLIAM CULLEN BRYANT - "THANATOPSIS" & "TO A WATERFOWL"

WEEK 16

MAKE IT REAL:

Try to find another example of an apostrophe in literature or poetry, or write an apostrophe yourself.

JAMES FENIMORE COOPER - FROM *THE LAST OF THE MOHICANS*
WILLIAM CULLEN BRYANT - "THANATOPSIS" & "TO A WATERFOWL"

WEEK 16

WRITING ASSIGNMENT:

This week you will write a literary critique comparing either the themes or the elements of Romanticism found in "Rip Van Winkle" and *The Last of the Mohicans*. (Only focus on one of these – not both.)
Complete *Write With the Best, Vol. 2* pages 47-49, Days 5-10.
Remember you are comparing one aspect of these two works. Make sure you follow the guidelines on pages 96-98.

JAMES FENIMORE COOPER - FROM *THE LAST OF THE MOHICANS*
WILLIAM CULLEN BRYANT - "THANATOPSIS" & "TO A WATERFOWL"

WEEK 16

CULMINATING ACTIVITY:

Read some or all of "Thanatopsis" out loud and have someone clap the rhythm of iambic pentameter. Pay close attention to the tone that this rhythm and blank verse create.

RALPH WALDO EMERSON - "THE AMERICAN SCHOLAR"
HENRY WADSWORTH LONGFELLOW - "A PSALM OF LIFE" & "A SLAVE'S DREAM"

WEEK 17

RALPH WALDO EMERSON

"In the degenerate state, when the victim of society, he tends to become a mere thinker, or still worse, the parrot of other men's thinking."

BACKGROUND CHECK:

1) Who is considered the most influential writer of the nineteenth century?

Ralph Waldo Emerson

2) What was Emerson's most famous essay?

"Self-Reliance"

3) Which college was Emerson banned from for three decades after speaking there twice?

Harvard

4) What was Emerson's profession at age 21?

Minister/ Pastor

5) What tragic event in his life caused him to finally and fully deny Christianity and totally embrace Transcendentalism?

The death of his wife

RALPH WALDO EMERSON - "THE AMERICAN SCHOLAR"
HENRY WADSWORTH LONGFELLOW - "A Psalm of Life" & "A Slave's Dream"

WEEK 17

RALPH WALDO EMERSON

WORDS TO KNOW:

Identify the part of speech of each word, and give one or two synonyms for each.

anomaly	Noun	deviation from normal or usual, aberration, departure, exception, inconsistency
antedate	Verb	occur or cause to occur earlier, accelerate, precede, pace, antecede
bibliomaniac	Noun	one who reads habitually, bookworm, bibliophile, reader
complaisant	Adj.	agreeable, accommodating, amiable, compliant, conciliatory, easy
dissipate	Verb	scatter, spread, disperse, dissolve, spend, consume, deplete, expend
enendator	Noun	one who critically emends or edits, one that makes textual corrections
fetish	Noun	obsession, bias, craze, mania, prejudice, object believed to have supernatural powers, charm, idol, image
nebulous	Adj.	confused, obscure, ambiguous, amorphous, cloudy, dark, dim, hazy
pecuniary	Adj.	financial, business, economic, fiscal, monetary, exchange, retail
refractory	Adj.	stubborn, headstrong, obstinate, unruly, firm, hard, rigid, stiff
satiety	Noun	satiation, filling, gratification, indulgence, surfeit
transmute	Verb	convert, alter, apply, appropriate, interchange, modify
undulation	Noun	wave, fluctuation, roll, sway
presentiment	Noun	anticipation, expectation, apprehension, disturbance, fear, forboding
indispensable	Adj.	necessary, basic, cardinal, crucial, essential, fundamental
auspicious	Adj.	encouraging, favorable, advantageous, bright, felicitous
indomitably	Adv.	obstinately, stubbornly, firmly, determinedly

| RALPH WALDO EMERSON - "THE AMERICAN SCHOLAR" HENRY WADSWORTH LONGFELLOW - "A PSALM OF LIFE" & "A SLAVE'S DREAM" | WEEK 17 |

RALPH WALDO EMERSON

LITERARY ANALYSIS:

American Renaissance: Time period in American Literature from 1850- 1855 where influential works from this period's major writers (Emerson, Thoreau, Hawthorne, Melville, and Whitman) were written. The works of these men helped the U.S. win literary independence from Great Britain.

Internal Rhyme: Rhyme occurring at the middle and end of a metrical line of poetry. Example: "To the rhyming and chiming of the bells!"

Free Verse: Verse that lacks regular meter and line length but relies upon natural rhythms.

CRITICAL READING QUESTIONS:

1) According to Emerson, the influence of the past comes to us best in what way?
**Books**

2) A scholar can change the shape of the world by changing the way men _see_ it.

3) Emerson says fear comes from what? _**Ignorance**_

4) The scholar in the right state is what kind of *man?* How does this man assert his intellectual independence?
**A thinking man or Man Thinking/ by thinking and learning outside the box**

5) What is the right use of books? _**To inspire**_

6) Why do you think this essay may have been controversial and radical during a time when education consisted mainly of rote learning and a limited prescribed curriculum?
**Emerson prescribed another way to look at education and scholarship, and mainly emphasized thinking.**

7) According to Emerson, can books be used in the wrong way? _**Yes**_

RALPH WALDO EMERSON - "THE AMERICAN SCHOLAR"
HENRY WADSWORTH LONGFELLOW - "A PSALM OF LIFE" & "A SLAVE'S DREAM"

WEEK 17

> *"Lives of great men all remind us, we can make our lives sublime, and, departing, leave behind us footsteps on the sands of time."*

HENRY WADSWORTH LONGFELLOW

BACKGROUND CHECK:

1) Longfellow was the first American poet to be enshrined where?
Westminster Abbey, Poet's Corner

2) Which American Writer did Longfellow admire the most? *Washington Irving*

3) Where was Longfellow a professor? *Harvard*

4) What controversial view did he write about in some of his poetry?
Anti-slavery view and politics

5) What happened to both of his wives? *They died tragically.*

6) Name 3 of his most famous narrative poems.
"The Song of Hiawantha", "Evangeline", "The Midnight Ride of Paul Revere", "The Courtship of Miles Standish"

7) (You will have to do research to answer this.)
Who were the Fireside Poets? *Bryant, Longfellow, Lowell, Holmes, and Whittier*
Why were they called this?
Their poetry was read by and written for families who sat by the fireside.

Read With the Best · Diagnostic Prescriptive Services | www.edudps.com

Ralph Waldo Emerson - "The American Scholar"
Henry Wadsworth Longfellow - "A Psalm of Life" & "A Slave's Dream"

Week 17

Henry Wadsworth Longfellow

Words To Know:

Identify the part of speech of each word, and give one or two synonyms for each.

earnest	Adj.	very enthusiastic, ardent, devoted, eager, fervent, fervid, sincere
bivouac	Noun	shelter for military, camp, headquarters, lodge
sublime	Adj.	great, magnificent, abstract, august, divine, elevated, eminent
scabbard	Noun	container, case, covering, bag, envelope, safe
tamarind	Noun	long-lived tropical evergreen or fruit
tempestuous	Adj.	wild, stormy, agitated, boisterous, coarse, emotional, excited
fetter	Verb Noun	tie up, hold, bind, chain, relish bindings, bondages

Ralph Waldo Emerson - "The American Scholar"
Henry Wadsworth Longfellow - "A Psalm of Life" & "A Slave's Dream"

Week 17

Henry Wadsworth Longfellow

Critical Reading Questions:

1) In "Psalm of Life", name two metaphors Longfellow uses to describe our journey in life. *A battlefield and ship voyage*

2) What is our "destined end or way"? Also refer to Stanza IX.
To act so that we accomplish something and progress each day, "up and doing and achieving and pursuing"

3) In "Psalm of Life", is Longfellow satisfied with the "status quo" or the ordinary? *No*

Give a line to prove your answer.
Examples: "Be not like dumb, driven cattle! Be a hero in the strife!"
"footsteps on the sands of time"

4) What is a famous metaphor in this poem?
"Footsteps on the sands of time"

5) Where is the slave sleeping in "The Slave's Dream" when his dream takes place?
A rice field where he is working

6) In "The Slave's Dream", name two examples of personification in stanza 7.
The tongues of the forest shouted, and the desert cried aloud.

7) In the last stanza, the slave's body is a worn-out what? *Fetter or chains*
What breaks it and throws it away? *his soul breaks it and throws it away*

8) Give two examples of internal rhyme in this poem.
"His breast was bare, his matted hair," "His bride-reins were golden chains"

Ralph Waldo Emerson - "The American Scholar"
Henry Wadsworth Longfellow - "A Psalm of Life" & "A Slave's Dream"

Week 17

Make It Real:

Find a copy of Emerson's "Concord Hymn" written as a memorial of the battle that started the Revolutionary War. Print a copy and try to memorize it, or at least memorize the stanza with the famous lines. Which lines are famous? Note that Emerson's grandfather actually witnessed this battle.
__Famous words are "the shot heard around the world."__

Ralph Waldo Emerson - "The American Scholar"
Henry Wadsworth Longfellow - "A Psalm of Life" & "A Slave's Dream"

Week 17

Writing Assignment:

You will begin learning how to write free verse poetry this week which is similar to blank verse with no rhyme but is not written in iambic pentameter. Free verse does not have a regular meter or line length like blank verse does. Complete Days 1-2 and 4 on pages 15-18 in *Write With The Best, Vol. 2*. You will already be familiar with most of these literary terms.

RALPH WALDO EMERSON - "THE AMERICAN SCHOLAR"
HENRY WADSWORTH LONGFELLOW - "A PSALM OF LIFE" & "A SLAVE'S DREAM"

WEEK 17

CULMINATING ACTIVITY:

Read "Psalm of Life" aloud with emphasis. As a group, assign students a stanza, and read this poem out loud using emphasis and fervor. Do you think "Psalm of Life" is a good title for this poem? Discuss your answer.
Opinion; answers will vary.

NATHANIEL HAWTHORNE
"Young Goodman Brown" & "The Minister's Black Veil"

WEEK 18

NATHANIEL HAWTHORNE

"The fiend in his own shape is less hideous, than when he rages in the breast of man."

BACKGROUND CHECK:

1) Is Hawthorne known for giving concrete interpretations in his fictional writings?

<u>No</u>

2) Who were Hawthorne's ancestors?

<u>Puritans</u>

3) Was Hawthorne able to support his young family with his writing?

<u>No</u>

4) Why was *The Scarlet Letter* denounced at first?

<u>For its treatment of adultery</u>

5) Why did *The Scarlet Letter* become a literary sensation in America and Great Britain?

<u>Brilliant prose and ability to recreate the past</u>

6) Why did Hawthorne write "The Custom House"?

<u>To get revenge against the Whigs' administration</u>

NATHANIEL HAWTHORNE
"Young Goodman Brown" & "The Minister's Black Veil"

WEEK 18

"YOUNG GOODMAN BROWN"
WORDS TO KNOW:

Identify the part of speech of each word, and give one or two synonyms for each.

ocular	Adj.	with the eye, sight, visible, visual
pendent	Adj.	dangling, droopy, hanging
festoon	Verb / Noun	decorate, adorn, hang, trim, / flower arrangement, decoration, corsage
proselyte	Noun	convert, disciple, follower, neophyte
fravity	Noun	force, pressure, weight, seriousness, importance, consequence, concern
mirth	Noun	great joy, amusement, cheer, frolic, entertainment
consorting	Verb	being friendly with, fraternizing, accompanying, associating
cognizance	Noun	understanding, acknowledgement, apprehension, attention
benignantly	Adv.	thoughtfully, affably, agreeably, attentively
abashed	Adj.	disconcerted, embarrassed, ashamed, bewildered, ill at ease, confounded
similitude	Noun	semblance, copy, likeness, replica, resemblance, counterpart
wanton	Adj.	extravagant, lustful, abandoned, lewd, cruel, malicious, arbitrary, evil
anathema	Noun	something hated, abomination, bane, enemy, condemnation

LITERARY ANALYSIS:

Prose: The ordinary form of written language without metrical (poetical) or rhythmic form.

Allegory: A story told in prose or poetry in which characters, actions, or settings represent ideas or qualities.
An allegory has a literal and symbolic meaning.
Example: *Pilgrim's Progress* by John Bunyan is a famous allegory.

Parable: A short, simple story that teaches a lesson.

NATHANIEL HAWTHORNE
"Young Goodman Brown" & "The Minister's Black Veil"

WEEK 18

"YOUNG GOODMAN BROWN"
CRITICAL READING QUESTIONS:

1) What is the setting of "Young Goodman Brown"?
1600's Salem, Massachusetts

What is the significance of this setting?
This is where the Salem Witch Trials took place.

2) After reading the story, what do you think is the significance of the names of the two main characters?
"Goodman" symbolizes a good man and "Faith" symbolizes the faith Goodman Brown is looking for and needs so desperately.

3) What does the traveler reveal to Goodman Brown when he says he comes from a long line of faithful Christians?
Brown's grandfather beat a Quaker woman, and his father burned an Indian village during King Philip's War.

4) Who is the traveler?
The Devil

5) What is the Biblical allusion concerning the staff?
It references the staff that the Egyptian magicians threw down when Moses cast the rod of God on the floor and it became a serpent. (Exodus 7:17)

6) What does the Devil say is the true nature of mankind and mankind's only happiness?
Evil

NATHANIEL HAWTHORNE
"Young Goodman Brown" & "The Minister's Black Veil"

Week 18

"YOUNG GOODMAN BROWN"
CRITICAL READING QUESTIONS (CONTINUED):

7) What does Goodman Brown ask Faith to do to resist the Devil?

Look towards heaven.

8) How could "Young Goodman Brown" be considered an allegory?

The characters stand for ideas and character traits, and the story has a literal and symbolic meaning.

9) Why is there no hopeful verse carved on Goodman Brown's tombstone, and why does his life become miserable?

He focuses on the sin and hypocrisy of other people and not on God and redemption through Jesus Christ; his life is a life of gloom and despair.

NATHANIEL HAWTHORNE
- "Young Goodman Brown" & "The Minister's Black Veil"

WEEK 18

"THE MINISTER'S BLACK VEIL"
WORDS TO KNOW:

Identify the part of speech of each word, and give one or two synonyms for each.

abash	Verb	embarrass, disconcert, annoy, confuse, disgrace
antipathy	Noun	strong dislike, disgust, abhorrence, animosity
ambiguity	Noun	uncertainty of meaning, doubt, enigma, obscurity
constituent	Adj. / Noun	component, part, basic, division, elemental, essential, factor / voting, citizen, official
decorous	Adj.	appropriate, suitable, becoming, befitting; coarse,
indecorous	Adj.	improper, rude
deputation	Noun	group of representatives, committee, delegation
expedient	Adj.	worthwhile, appropriate, advantageous, beneficial, OR: Noun; resource, contrivance, device
mitigate	Verb	check, diminish, lighten, abate, allay, aid, support
ostentatious	Adj	flashy, showy, boastful, classy, conspicuous, dashing
pathos	Noun	deep sadness, desolation, emotion, feeling, passion
perturbation	Noun	distress, anxiety, commotion, confusion, disorder, clamor, uproar
portend	Verb	foreshadow, indicate, adumbrate, augur, forecast, omen
remonstrance	Noun	protest, complaint, objection, rebuke, reproach
solicitude	Noun	worry, anxiety, attention, care, concern, compunction
synod	Noun	council, assembly, body, committee, meeting
torpor	Noun	lethargy, apathy, laziness, sloth, slumber
unwonted	Adj.	unusual, abnormal, amazing, astonishing, atypical
vagary	Noun	caprice, fancy, humor, idea, impulse, inconsistency
imbued	Verb	infused, saturated, diffused, permeated
waggery	Noun	mischief, trouble, damage, wrong, transgression

Read With the Best
Diagnostic Prescriptive Services | www.edudps.com

NATHANIEL HAWTHORNE
"Young Goodman Brown" & "The Minister's Black Veil"

Week 18

"THE MINISTER'S BLACK VEIL"
CRITICAL READING QUESTIONS:

1) What does the black veil symbolize?
The separation that sin causes from people and God and/or the hidden sins of all humans

2) How does Hooper's congregation react to the veil?
They are amazed and somewhat irritated.

3) How does Elizabeth react to the veil at first and later?
She does not react the same as the people and asks him why he wears it. After he refuses to remove it, she becomes fearful.

4) What does Hooper sacrifice in human relationships because he refuses to take off the veil?
Elizabeth does not marry him, children avoid him, and he does not receive love or sympathy from people.

5) How is the story a parable? *It teaches a moral lesson.*

6) Is the veil ever removed from Hooper's face? *No*

7) What was the "saddest of all prisons"? *Hooper's own heart*

8) How is Minister Hooper a lot like Young Goodman Brown?
They both focus on the darkness and sin in people instead of hope and redemption, and this changes them.

9) Do you agree with Hooper that every visage has a black veil?
Opinion

Nathaniel Hawthorne
"Young Goodman Brown" & "The Minister's Black Veil"

WEEK 18

MAKE IT REAL:

Does Hawthorne appear to be an optimist or pessimist? How do you support this answer?
Opinion

Nathaniel Hawthorne
"Young Goodman Brown" & "The Minister's Black Veil"

Week 18

Writing Assignment:

You will write a poem this week in free verse on a subject of your choice. If you are brave, you may attempt blank verse (iambic pentameter).
Look at *Write With The Best, Vol. 2*, Days 6-10, pages 18-19.
Proofread your poem by using the checklists on pages 104 and 114.

Culminating Activity:

Alone or in a group, find at least 2 literary devices Hawthorne uses in his stories.
Answers will vary.

NATHANIEL HAWTHORNE
- THE SCARLET LETTER (CHAPTERS 1-4)

WEEK 19

"But the point which drew all eyes and, as it were, transfigured the wearer ... was that scarlet letter, so fantastically embroidered and illuminated upon her bosom."

NATHANIEL HAWTHORNE

WORDS TO KNOW:

Identify the part of speech of each word, and give one or two synonyms for each.

inauspicious	Adj.	negative, unlucky, ominous, threatening
augured	Verb	portended, forecasted, prophesied, read
indubitably	Adv.	certainly, apparently, unassailably
heterodox	Adj.	having opinions that oppose those of the church or accepted doctrine, rebellious, blasphemous
infamy	Noun	disgrace, dishonor, shame, fame for criminal activity
farthingale	Noun	a support, such as a hoop, worn beneath a skirt to extend it horizontally from the waist, used by European women in the 16th and 17th centuries.
evanescent	Adj.	transient, ephemeral, fleeting, fugitive
ignominy	Noun	disgrace, dishonor, degradation, debasement
contumely	Noun	arrogance, rudeness
remonstrance	Noun	objection, complaint, expostulation
wont	Adj.	in the habit of, accustomed, given, inclined, used
physiognomies	Noun	visages, expressions, divinations
antinomian	Noun	a person who believes that all that the only virtue needed for salvation is one's faith in God
malefactress	Noun	criminal, offender, felon, culprit, female evil-doer
sumptuary	Adj.	regulatory, limiting
heterogeneous	Adj.	miscellaneous, mixed, varied, motley, assorted, diverse

NATHANIEL HAWTHORNE
- The Scarlet Letter (Chapters 1-4)

WEEK 19

Words To Know (continued):

congenial	Adj.	naturally suited, similar in tastes and habits, favorable, agreeable, compatible
rotundity	Noun	resonance, vibrance, strength, corpulence, obesity
purport	Noun	importance, intension, purpose, meaning
mien	Noun	manner, demeanor, expression, style, characteristic
sagacity	Noun	shrewdness, intelligence, wisdom, knowledge, perspicacity
plaintive	Adj.	sad, lamenting, mournful, melancholy
quell	Verb	to subdue, to crush, suppress, pacify, quiet, quash, stifle
peremptory	Adj.	absolute and final, commanding, conclusive, decisive, self-assured, dominating
efficacy	Noun	effectiveness, efficiency, potency
expostulation	Noun	an expression of opposition, reasoning, argument, dissuasion, assertion, remonstration

Use 3 of the "Words to Know" to describe the character of Hester Prynne.
Answers will vary.

_____

_____

_____

_____

Literary Analysis:

Foreshadowing: A showing, indication, or suggestion of what is to occur later in a literary work.

NATHANIEL HAWTHORNE
- THE SCARLET LETTER (CHAPTERS 1-4)

WEEK 19

CRITICAL READING QUESTIONS:

1) What is the setting of *The Scarlet Letter*?
17th century Boston

2) What is the occupation of the narrator of this story? (Hint: Refer to "The Custom House" at the beginning of the book)
Customs officer

3) What is the purpose of the rosebush that grows outside the prison door? What element of Romanticism do you see in Hawthorne using the rosebush?
To provide "a sweet moral blossom" or some relief for sorrow and gloom and a reminder of Nature's kindness to the condemned; the element of Nature

4) Why is Hester Prynne being punished, and what is her punishment?
She has committed adultery; she must stand in the town square for public humiliation and wear a scarlet letter "A" sewn on her dress for the rest of her life.

5) What do the Puritan magistrates hope to accomplish by punishing Hester this way?
They hope to deter others from committing the same sin.

6) What criticism do the women give about the scarlet letter Hester is wearing?
They say it is too fancy and ornate; they also think it isn't punishment.

7) Whom does Hester recognize in the crowd that surprises and frightens her as she stands on the scaffold?
Her husband, Roger Chillingworth

NATHANIEL HAWTHORNE
- THE SCARLET LETTER (CHAPTERS 1-4)

WEEK 19

CRITICAL READING QUESTIONS (CONTINUED):

8) Why has Chillingworth been delayed in coming to Boston?
He was captured by Indians.

9) What do you think Chillingworth's name indicates about his character?
He is cold and unfeeling and devoid of human warmth.

10) What question does Chillingworth ask Hester when he comes to visit her in prison?
He asks who Hester's partner in adultery was.

11) At the end of Chapter 4, Hester asks Chillingworth if he is going to entice her into a bond of secrecy that will ruin her soul, and Chillingworth replies, "Not thy soul….no, not thine!" What do you think Hawthorne is foreshadowing in this statement?
That he is seeking the ruin of someone else's soul – possibly the person she committed adultery with

Nathaniel Hawthorne
- The Scarlet Letter (Chapters 1-4)

Week 19

Make It Real:

Find out what Hester's punishment for adultery would have been in real Puritan Boston. *__She could have been whipped severely or put to death.__*

Writing Assignment:

You will begin this week to learn how to write an efficient business letter. Complete Days 1-2 in *Write With the Best, Vol. 2*, pages 20-22.

Note: You will not actually write the letter this week.

Nathaniel Hawthorne
- The Scarlet Letter (Chapters 1-4)

Week 19

CULMINATING ACTIVITY:

Three of the four main characters have been introduced this week – Hester, Pearl, and Chillingworth.
Choose one or all of these characters, and come up with a brief commercial selling yourself as a character.
Tell about yourself so far and what we can expect from you throughout the rest of the novel.

NATHANIEL HAWTHORNE
- THE SCARLET LETTER (CHAPTERS 5-8)

WEEK 20

"Continually, and in a thousand other ways, did she feel innumerable throbs of anguish that had been so cunningly contrived for her by the undying, the ever active sentence of the Puritan tribunal."

NATHANIEL HAWTHORNE

LITERARY ANALYSIS:

Irony: A technique in literature of indicating an intention or attitude different than what is actually stated.

Situational Irony: When events end up the opposite of what is expected.

Dramatic Irony: Facts or situations that are different than what is expected and are known to the readers but not to the characters.

Paradox: A self-contradictory or absurd statement that is actually true.

Example: Jesus said, "He who saves his life will lose it, and he who loses his life for My sake will find it."

NATHANIEL HAWTHORNE
- The Scarlet Letter (Chapters 5-8)

Week 20

WORDS TO KNOW:

Identify the part of speech of each word, and give one or two synonyms for each.

lurid	Adj.	harshly shocking, revolting, glowing, ghastly, gruesome, fiery
inscrutable	Adj.	mysterious, impenetrable, cryptic, enigmatic
uncongenial	Adj.	unsuitable, unfavorable, disagreeable, incompatible, unpleasurable
incurred	Verb	became liable, got, obtained, endured, sustained
progenitor	Noun	a direct ancestor, forerunner, predecessor, forefather
ascetic	Adj.	self-denying, abstinent, austere, continent, temperature
ingenuity	Adj.	cleverness, intensiveness, imagination, creativity
repugnance	Noun	strong dislike, distaste or antagonism, repulsion, aversion
succor	Verb	to give or to offer relief, aid, help, support
alchemy	Noun	hermeticsm, magic, pseudo-science
prolific	Adj.	productive, generative, fertile, teeming, bountiful, fruitful
insidious	Adj.	treacherous, devious, deceitful, perfidious
procured	Verb	obtained, acquired, secured, got, gained
sullied	Verb	soiled, tarnished, stained, tainted, defiled, marred
talisman	Noun	lucky charm, amulet, idol
averred	Verb	affirmed, attested, asserted
imbued	Verb	permeated, moistened, wet, dyed
caprice	Noun	an impulsive change of mind, fickleness, whim
conjuration	Noun	materialization, spell, charm, recollection
anathemas	Noun	aversions, bans, excrations, horrors, abominations
perpetuated	Verb	sustained, preserved, continued, lived on
sportive	Adj.	frolicsome, playful, frisky, merry, lively
imperious	Adj.	overbearing, domineering, despotic, authoritarian
dauntless	Adj.	fearless, intimidated, brave, courageous, unafraid
tome	Noun	volume, codex, a book (usually large and academic)
ponderous	Adj.	weighty, heavy, large, hefty, massive, cumbersome, unwieldy
exigence	Noun	a demand or requirement, emergency, necessity, crisis, urgency
antiquated	Adj.	outdated, obsolete, archaic, old-fashioned
indefeasible	Adj.	not able to be voided or undone, decisive, permanent
singular	Adj.	uncommon, peculiar, unusual, odd, rare, unique, individual
adduced	Verb	alleged, proposed, urged, promoted, furthered
comely	Adj.	attractive, becoming, pretty
cabalistic	Adj.	cryptic, having secret meaning

NATHANIEL HAWTHORNE
- THE SCARLET LETTER (CHAPTERS 5-8)

WEEK 20

WORDS TO KNOW (CONTINUED):

Use 3 of the "Words to Know" to describe Pearl.
Answers will vary.

_____

_____

_____

CRITICAL READING QUESTIONS:

1) How does Hester support herself financially? *She does needlework for the town.*
What is the only public ceremony she cannot participate in? *a wedding*

2) What is the significance of Pearl's name?
She was her mother's greatest treasure, and she was purchased with a great price.

3) What example of situational irony do you discover about Pearl's character and the effect she has on Hester's life?
She is both a sign of Hester's sin and shame and her greatest treasure.

4) Where does Hester live after she is released from prison?
In a small cottage on the outskirts of town away from the houses

5) How many years have passed since the opening chapter of the book? *3 years*

6) In Chapter 7, what colors does Hawthorne use to describe Pearl?
"dark glossy brown", "crimson and gold", "fiery luster", "black shadow", "deeply black eyes", "small black mirror of Pearl's eyes"
What do these colors symbolize?
red symbolizes passion, and black symbolizes sin.

Nathaniel Hawthorne
- The Scarlet Letter (Chapters 5-8)

Week 20

CRITICAL READING QUESTIONS (CONTINUED):

7) What are the two reasons Hester goes to Governor Bellingham's mansion?
To deliver a pair of gloves she made and to find out if the magistrates intend on taking Pearl from her

8) How does Pearl respond when she is asked who made her?
She says she was not born but plucked from a rose bush outside the prison's door.

9) How is Pearl dressed, and how is this significant?
Pearl is dressed also in an elaborate red dress with gold embroidery. Her dress is contrary to Puritan dress, and she is also bearing the shame of her mother.

10) Who argues for Pearl to remain with Hester?
Reverend Dimmesdale

11) What is the one beautiful plant that grows in Governor Bellingham's garden?
A rosebush

12) What is paradoxical and ironic about Mistress Hibbins, the Governor's sister?
She is an admitted witch, but a protected member of the community, whereas Hester, who sinned once, is an outcast and may lose her child.

NATHANIEL HAWTHORNE
- THE SCARLET LETTER (CHAPTERS 5-8)

WEEK 20

MAKE IT REAL:

After reading these chapters and thinking of *The Scarlet Letter* as a type of allegory, what do you think Governor Bellingham and Reverend Wilson are symbols of? What do they represent?

Answer:
Governor Bellingham: The state or government
Reverend Wilson: The church

Read With the Best

Nathaniel Hawthorne
- The Scarlet Letter (Chapters 5-8)

Week 20

WRITING ASSIGNMENT:

This week you will write a business letter to the magistrate in Boston telling him you disagree with Hester's punishment and treatment. You are to tell him what changes should be made.
Complete Days 3 and 5-10 in *Write With The Best, Vol. 2,* pages 22-24.
(You also need to start thinking about a topic for your research paper you will be writing on any American author, work of literature or literary period (such as Romanticism) in this curriculum.)

NATHANIEL HAWTHORNE
- The Scarlet Letter (Chapters 5-8)

WEEK 20

CULMINATING ACTIVITY:

Alone or as a group activity, come up with as many paradoxes as you can think of in 5 minutes.

Also, discuss real life situations that end up being both a blessing and a curse like Pearl.

NATHANIEL HAWTHORNE
- THE SCARLET LETTER (CHAPTERS 9-12)

WEEK 21

NATHANIEL HAWTHORNE

"But the point which drew all eyes and, as it were, transfigured the wearer ... was that scarlet letter, so fantastically embroidered and illuminated upon her bosom."

WORDS TO KNOW:

Identify the part of speech of each word, and give one or two synonyms for each.

appellation	Noun	title or name, denomination, designation, tag, moniker
infamy	Noun	disgrace, dishonor, shame
ponderous	Adj.	weighty, hefty, large, heavy, massive, cumbersome
boon	Noun	windfall, favor, treasure, benefit
scrupulous	Adj.	conscientious, painstaking, meticulous, punctilious
query	Noun	question, inquiry, interrogation
importunate	Adj.	craving, beseeching, earnest, imperative, troublesome, persistent
stifled	Adj.	stuffy, muted, muffled, restrained
orthodox	Adj.	conventional, standard, customary, accepted, conservative, traditional
efficacy	Noun	potency, effectiveness, efficiency
affinity	Noun	similarity, resemblance, partiality, agreement, fondness
erudition	Noun	knowledge, education
commodiousness	Noun	roominess, spaciousness, largeness
conjurer	Noun	sorcerer, magician, illusionist
ominous	Adj.	menacing, threatening, indicating, misfortune, inauspicious, dire, sinister
stealthily	Adv.	cautiously, quietly, furtively, secretly, covertly, scrumptiously
inimical	Adj.	hostile, unfriendly, injurious, harmful, adverse
propagate	Verb	reproduce, procreate, distribute, circulate
penitential	Adj.	remorseful, apologetic, repentant
abasement	Noun	shame, disgrace, corruption, humiliation
decorously	Adv.	politely, courteously, appropriately
whimsy	Noun	notion, fantasy, impulse, outburst, bout

Read With the Best   Diagnostic Prescriptive Services | www.edudps.com

NATHANIEL HAWTHORNE
THE SCARLET LETTER (CHAPTERS 9-12)

WEEK 21

WORDS TO KNOW (CONTINUED):

Use 4 of the "Words to Know" to describe Dimmesdale's suffering.
Answers will vary.

_____

_____

_____

LITERARY ANALYSIS:

Crisis: Extreme conflict of a plot in a novel, story, poem, or play which leads to the climax.

Climax: The turning point in a play, novel, poem, or short story in which a crisis comes to its point of greatest intensity and is, in some manner, resolved. There is usually one major climax in a literary work, but there can also be minor climaxes.

CRITICAL READING QUESTIONS:

1) Why is Chillingworth so readily accepted as the town doctor? *The townspeople do not have good medical care, and they want help for Dimmesdale.*

2) What is the common title given to doctors during this time? *The leech*
Why is this an especially appropriate title for Chillingworth.
he sucks the life out of Dimmesdale and attaches himself to him.

3) What hangs on the walls of Dimmesdale's library? *A tapestry of David and Bathsheba who committed adultery and Nathan the prophet*

4) What was Chillingworth trying to say to Dimmesdale by telling him about the herbs he gathered from a grave? *He was referring to Dimmesdale's own hideous secret that was buried with him.*

5) How does Chillingworth's appearance begin to change? *His face became distorted*

NATHANIEL HAWTHORNE
- *THE SCARLET LETTER* (CHAPTERS 9-12)

WEEK 21

CRITICAL READING QUESTIONS (CONTINUED):

6) What climax takes place at the end of Chapter 10? *Chillingworth discovers something on Dimmesdale's chest that appears to reveal his guilt.*

7) Why does Dimmesdale start to deliver his most powerful sermons?
He can relate to the suffering and sin of his parishioners

8) Name three ways that Dimmesdale thinks he can pay and tries to pay for his sins.
He whips himself, he fasts, he holds extended vigils, and he meditates on his sin.

9) Where does Dimmesdale decide to go to try and alleviate his pain? *The scaffold*

10) What symbol does the meteor produce in the sky? *The letter A*
What do the townspeople interpret this to mean?
they say it stands for Angel to represent the Governor who has died
What does Dimmesdale think it means? *Adultery*

11) What crisis in this novel is brought to a climax in chapters 11 and 12?
Dimmesdale's spiritual and moral crisis

12) What is the ironic and symbolic meaning of the scaffold for Hester and Dimmesdale?
Hester had public torment on it, and Dimmesdale has inner torment on it.

13) Who do you think suffers more from the results of sin- Hester or Dimmesdale?
Opinion
Do you think Dimmesdale would have been better off to reveal his sin 7 years earlier as Hester was forced to? *Opinion*

Read With the Best

NATHANIEL HAWTHORNE
- THE SCARLET LETTER (CHAPTERS 9-12)

WEEK 21

MAKE IT REAL:

Think of other examples in literature where bitterness and hatred in a person have possibly altered or changed his or her appearance as Chillingworth's appearance was changed.

_____

_____

_____

WRITING ASSIGNMENT:

You will begin the process of choosing and narrowing a topic for your research paper this week. Your topic must relate to your study of American literature this year. You may choose any author, literary work, or literary time period such as Romanticism or Transcendentalism. (See list of suggested topics.)
Read pages 7-16 in *Writing A Research Paper: A Step-by-Step Approach*.
Complete exercises 4, 5, and 8 only. These will teach you how to narrow a topic for a research paper. Also, see the schedule on page 152 for completing your research paper in the next 12 weeks. This schedule is different from the one in the book.

Example Research Paper Topics

1. Symbolism in Herman Melville's works
2. Figurative language in Edward Taylor's poetry
3. Benjamin Franklin's writing style
4. The stereotypes of James Fenimore Cooper
5. The themes of Emily Dickinson's poetry
6. The influence of Sojourner Truth's writings and speeches
7. How Phillis Wheatley's life influenced her poetry
8. Nathaniel Hawthorne's Puritan ancestry revealed in his writings
9. Anne Bradstreet's view of marriage and children demonstrated in her writings
10. The writing style and dominant themes of Mary Rowlandson's writing
11. The themes of Jonathan Edward's works
12. The influence of Romanticism in 18th century American writing
13. Major conflicts in the writings of Edgar Allen Poe
14. The symbolism of Nathaniel Hawthorne
15. The stereotypes of Washington Irving
16. The influence of Thoreau's *Walden* on American culture
17. Poe's life revealed in his writing
18. The themes of Henry Wadsworth Longfellow
19. The influence of the letters of John and Abigail Adams
20. How Thomas Paine's writings changed the world

NATHANIEL HAWTHORNE
The Scarlet Letter (Chapters 9-12)

Week 21

Completing Your Research Paper

Week:	Step:
21	1. Choose a topic and narrow it.
22	2. Find sources for topic and revise topic if necessary.
23	3. Continue to find sources by visiting the library and make bibliography cards.
24	4. Write a thesis statement and title.
25	5. Write a tentative outline and start taking notes.
26	6. Take notes.
27	7. Take notes.
28	8. Take notes.
29	9. Revise outline and start rough draft.
30	10. Write rough draft and revise.
31	11. Type paper and bibliography page.
32	12. Proofread paper and make revisions.
33	13. Turn in paper to be graded.

Research Paper Checklist (Each item counts 10 point.)
Reproducible copy can be found in the back of the Teacher's Edition.

- ☐ The subject pertains to our literary study and is narrowed into a manageable topic.

- ☐ There is a clear thesis statement in the first paragraph.

- ☐ There is an outline.

- ☐ It is evident that adequate research has been done. (It is a <u>research</u> paper, not a report, and not an opinionated essay.)

- ☐ Works are cited correctly <u>within</u> the paper.

- ☐ There is no noticeable plagiarism. Everyone else's ideas have been cited or referenced.

- ☐ There is a "Works Cited" page done correctly.

- ☐ There is unity throughout - Every main idea of every paragraph relates to the thesis statement, and there is a topic sentence for every paragraph.

- ☐ There are not many spelling or grammar errors - no more than 4 or 5. (The paper has been proofread adequately.)

- ☐ There is an adequate conclusion.

NATHANIEL HAWTHORNE
The Scarlet Letter (Chapters 9-12)

WEEK 21

CULMINATING ACTIVITY:

Alone or in a group, come up with a different minor climax than the one in Chapters 11 and 12. Act out this climax and the results of it.

Nathaniel Hawthorne
The Scarlet Letter (Chapters 13-16)

Week 22

NATHANIEL HAWTHORNE

> *"'Mother,' said little Pearl, 'the sunshine does not love you. It runs away and hides itself, because it is afraid of something on your bosom.'"*

Words To Know:

Identify the part of speech of each word, and give one or two synonyms for each.

abase	Verb	shame, humiliate, disgrace
faculty	Noun	aptitude, capability, sense, skill
repose	Noun	sleep, rest, ease, calmness, serenity, relaxation
gibe	Verb	ridicule, mockery, derision, jeer, jab
despotic	Adj.	tyrannical, oppressive, dictatorial, authoritarian
luxuriant	Adj.	lavish, arrogant, rich, abundant, profuse
stigmatize	Verb	scandalize, denounce, brand, mark with disgrace
quietude	Noun	peace, tranquility, calm, ease, serenity
obviate	Verb	eliminate, preclude, wert, forestall, deter, to prevent or make unnecessary
acquiesce	Verb	submitted, acceded, consented, agreed
misgiving	Noun	distrust, qualm, presentiment, disquiet
perpetration	Noun	wrongdoing, action, performance
bane	Noun	curse, scourge, poison, plague
verdure	Noun	greenery, foliage, woodedness, immaturity
sedulous	Adj.	persistent, careful, attentive, diligent
upbraid	Verb	berate, reproach, rebuke, chide
impalpable	Adj.	unreal, intangible, imperceptible, tenuous, unsubstantial
founder	Verb	immerse, plunge, sink, fall helplessly
capricious	Adj.	erratic, fickle, flighty, inconsistent, wayward
precocity	Noun	brightness, talent, aptitude
acrid	Adj.	harsh, bitter, sharp, pungent
asperity	Noun	harshness, meanness, sharpness, irritability, crossness
impute	Verb	attribute, ascribe, credit
scintillate	Verb	sparkle, flash, gleam, glisten, glimmer, shimmer, twinkle
loquacity	Noun	talkativeness, garrulousness, verbosity, wordiness

NATHANIEL HAWTHORNE
- *THE SCARLET LETTER* (CHAPTERS 13-16)

WEEK 22

WORDS TO KNOW (CONTINUED):

cadence	Noun	*measure, beat, tempo, meter*
vivacious	*Adj.*	*lively, spirited, animated, dynamic, vibrant, zesty*
listlessness	Noun	*lethargy, sluggishness, languor, indolence*

LITERARY ANALYSIS:

Conflict: In fiction, the opposition of persons or forces upon which the action and plot depend.

There are basically three types of conflict, and some literary works have a combination of all three.

Physical conflict: This is the struggle between man and the physical world including nature in any form.

Social conflict: This is the struggle between man and man, man and society, or man and fate or destiny. This includes racial and religious prejudices.

Internal or psychological conflict: This is the struggle between desires within a person, which creates inner turmoil.

CRITICAL READING QUESTIONS:

1) As time passes, what do the townspeople begin to believe the "A" on Hester's chest means? *"Able"*

What are some of Hester's actions that cause the people to change their minds about her? *She gives food to the poor, nurses the sick, and aids those in trouble.*

2) How does Hester say the scarlet letter will be removed?
Divine Providence will make it fall from her chest when it is time.

3) When Hester tries to convince Chillingworth to relent his revenge and tells him she will reveal his identity to Dimmesdale, what is Chillingworth's reply?
He replies that this is their fate

What does this say about Chillingworth's character? *he does not take responsibility for his actions, but makes excuses.*

Nathaniel Hawthorne
The Scarlet Letter (Chapters 13-16)

Week 22

CRITICAL READING QUESTIONS (CONTINUED):

4) What has happened to Hester's appearance?
Even though she is kind and helpful to others, she has lost her femininity and become austere and has lost the hope of love.

5) Does Hester tell Pearl the truth about the scarlet letter? *No*

6) What happens to Hester and Pearl as they walk near the sunshine in the forest?
The sunshine disappears when Hester comes near it and remains on Pearl when she approaches it.
What does the light or sunshine symbolize? *Truth, innocence*

7) How does Pearl demonstrate her perceptiveness about the scarlet letter and Dimmesdale? *She asks why he always holds his hand over his heart, which is where the scarlet letter is sewn on her mother.*

8) What might the forest symbolize in this novel?
Liberality, the wild and natural, privacy, intimacy, secret sins, escape

9) List one example in this novel of physical conflict, social conflict and internal conflict.
Answers will vary, but one example of each is:
1) Social conflict: The conflict between Hester and society
2) Physical conflict: Dimmesdale and his illness
3) Internal conflict: Dimmesdale's struggle with his hidden sin

Read With the Best

NATHANIEL HAWTHORNE
The Scarlet Letter (Chapters 13-16)

WEEK 22

MAKE IT REAL:

Think of an example of one of the types of conflict in a famous book or movie. How is this conflict resolved? How does this conflict affect the plot and theme?
Answers will vary.

Nathaniel Hawthorne
- *The Scarlet Letter* (Chapters 13-16)

Week 22

WRITING ASSIGNMENT:

This week you will begin to look for resources for your topic you have chosen and revise your topic if necessary, according to the number of sources you can find for your topic. Before locating resources, read pages 22 to the top of 27 in *Writing a Research Paper*.

Complete exercises 1 and 5 only.

Please Note: You will need at least 5 sources for your paper and only 2-3 of these can be Internet sources.

This week you should find as many sources as you can on your topic, including locating library sources online, possibly putting a hold on these items, and locating Internet sources. Next week you will make a visit to the library to pick up your sources. If you have a college or university in your town, you may want to check with this library also.

Nathaniel Hawthorne
- *The Scarlet Letter* (Chapters 13-16)

Week 22

CULMINATING ACTIVITY:

Alone or in groups, pick one example of conflict Hawthorne uses in *The Scarlet Letter* and act it out, play charades, create a song to portray it, or illustrate it on paper. Have the audience guess the conflict. Then explain how Hawthorne uses this specific conflict to create tension and add complexity to his characters and how he uses it to develop the overall plot.

Nathaniel Hawthorne
- The Scarlet Letter (Chapters 17-20)

Week 23

NATHANIEL HAWTHORNE

"Of penance, I have had enough! Of penitence, there has been none! Else I should long ago have thrown off these garments of mock holiness and have shown myself to mankind as they will see me at the judgment seat."

Words To Know:

Identify the part of speech of each word, and give one or two synonyms for each.

epoch	Noun	period, era, generation, date
estrange	Verb	disaffected, separated, divorced
misanthropy	Noun	cynicism, pessimism
malignity	Noun	bitterness, resentment, malevolence
satiate	Verb	sate, cloy, glut, gorge
vestige	Noun	trace, remnant, relic, token, remains
renowned	Adj.	famed, eminent, prestigious, distinguished
requite	Verb	compensate, reimburse, revenge, pay back
minuteness	Noun	accuracy, exactness, carefulness, smallness
extenuation	Noun	mitigation, lightening
harrow	Verb	torment, terrify, agonize, upset, disturb, frighten, dismay
machination	Noun	plot, scheme, conspiracy, intrigue, design
breach	Noun	gap, lapse, rift; contravention, dereliction
grovel	Verb	cringe, fawn, kowtow, bootlick
denizen	Noun	resident, citizen, inhabitant
choleric	Adj.	irritable, surly, wrathful, irate
medium (n)	Noun	means, instrument, vehicle, mechanism
imperious	Adj.	authoritarian, despotic, domineering, overbearing
gesticulate	Verb	motion, indicate, signal
reproachfully	Adv.	disapprovingly, shamefully, meanly, abusively
caprice	Noun	an impulsive change of mind, fickleness, whim
talisman	Noun	lucky charm, amulet, idol
duplicity	Noun	duality, two-facedness, infidelity, disloyalty
disquietude	Noun	anxiety, edginess, uneasiness
acute	Adj.	clever, shrew, sharp, severe, keen, ingenious, intense, fierce

NATHANIEL HAWTHORNE
- THE SCARLET LETTER (CHAPTERS (17-20)

WEEK 23

WORDS TO KNOW (CONTINUED):

importunately	Adv.	beseechingly, earnestly, imperatively
mutability	Noun	changeability, inconsistency, impermanence
rapturously	Adv.	blissfully, delightfully
pithy	Adj.	brief, compact, concise, succinct
volley (n)	Noun	rupture, outburst, explosion; discharge, barrage, salvo, fusillade, hail
requisite	Adj.	essential, necessary, required, indispensable

LITERARY ANALYSIS:

Rising action: The part of a plot that involves complication and conflict and leads to the climax or turning point in a novel or play.

CRITICAL READING QUESTIONS:

1) What is different about the encounter between Hester and Dimmesdale in the forest?
It shows them in an intimate or close setting for the first time.

2) Why does Dimmesdale say that Chillingworth's sin was the worst of all?
"He has violated, in cold blood, the sanctity of a human heart". Chillingworth has hurt another human being, but he says he and Hester did not.
Do you agree or disagree? *Opinion*

3) What does Hester do to show that she has placed the past and her problems behind her? *She removes the scarlet letter and lets down her hair.*

4) What did Hester and Dimmesdale plan to do? *Move to Europe with Pearl*

5) "Of penance I have had enough! Of penitence there has been none!"
What does Dimmesdale mean by these words? *He means he has had outward acts of being sorry but has not truly repented in his heart, or he would have confessed his sin and stepped down from being a pastor.*
Do you agree or disagree? *Opinion*

Nathaniel Hawthorne
The Scarlet Letter (Chapters 17-20)

Week 23

CRITICAL READING QUESTIONS (CONTINUED):

6) What were Hester's teachers during the years she wore the scarlet letter?
Shame, Despair, Solitude
Did Hester truly repent? *No*
Did Hester believe it was okay to sin if it made you happy? *Yes*

7) Cite 3 examples of personification in the last two paragraphs of Chapter 18.
Answers will vary, but may include: "The great black forest had a playmate, was stern, etc." "the partridge repented," "flowers whispered"

8) Why will Pearl not come to Hester when she calls her?
Hester looks different – she is not wearing the scarlet letter, and her hair is down.
What does Hester do to make Pearl come? *She puts her scarlet letter back on.*

9) Name one example that Hawthorne gives to make his readers associate the truth and perception with Pearl. *Pearl asks if she and Hester and Dimmesdale can walk into town together holding hands; Pearl does not respond to her mother after she and Dimmesdale make their plans.*

10) Why do you think that Dimmesdale is tempted to commit various sins on his walk home after his encounter with Hester in the forest?
Answers will vary, but one main reason may be that now that he has chosen to continue to commit adultery with Hester, he has opened the door to many other sins, and he is tempted more.

NATHANIEL HAWTHORNE
- The Scarlet Letter (Chapters (17-20)

Week 23

MAKE IT REAL:

Think of a public or Biblical example where someone appeared sorry for a wrong they had done, but proved later it was not true repentance or penitence.
<u>Answers will vary.</u>

NATHANIEL HAWTHORNE
- THE SCARLET LETTER (CHAPTERS (17-20)

WEEK 23

WRITING ASSIGNMENT:

This week you will go to the library or libraries and check out sources for your research paper. You will also write your bibliography cards. You will need small or large index cards to do this.
Read carefully pages 35-42 in *Writing a Research Paper*.

Complete Exercise 13, odd numbers only.

You will be using MLA style for this paper.

Nathaniel Hawthorne
The Scarlet Letter (Chapters 17-20)

CULMINATING ACTIVITY:

Alone or in a group, create a commercial for a sitcom called "Hester Prynne" in which you introduce all the major events in her life outlined so far in the rising action of the novel.

Nathaniel Hawthorne
- The Scarlet Letter (Chapters 21-24)

Week 24

"But in the lapse of the toilsome, thoughtful, and self-devoted years that make up Hester's life, the scarlet letter ceased to be a stigma..."

NATHANIEL HAWTHORNE

Words To Know:

Identify the part of speech of each word, and give one or two synonyms for each.

plebian	Adj.	low-class, crude, vulgar, unrefined, coarse, common
requisite	Adj.	essential, necessary, required, indispensable
impracticable	Adj.	imprudent impossible, blocked, impassible
jocularity	Noun	joking, merriment, humorous fun
interposition	Noun	encroachment, intrusion, interference
ferocity	Noun	fickleness, violence, fury, vehemence, turbulence
arraign	Verb	accuse, challenge, denounce, inculpate
mercenary	Adj.	venal, materialistic, avaricious
burnished	Adj.	shiny, buffed, polished
inducement	Noun	motive, urging, encouragement, incentive
ominously	Adv	sinisterly, threateningly, menacingly
intangibility	Noun	illusory, impalpability, elusiveness, invisibility, abstraction
renown	Noun	fame, widespread acclaim, celebrity, prestige, standing, eminence
gradation	Noun	subtlety, nuance, shade, step
languidly	Adj.	slowly, sluggishly, weakly, listlessly
boorish	Adj.	vulgar, impolite, gruff, uncivilized
surmise	Verb	conjecture, speculate, infer
zenith	Noun	highest point, summit, acme, apex, climax, crown, pinnacle
etherealize	Verb	spiritualize, to become or make heavenly
conjectural	Adj.	doubtful, speculative, surmised, tentative, supposed
lurid	Adj.	revolting, harshly shocking, ghastly, garish, gruesome, grisly, glowing, fiery, macabre
transmute	Verb	transform, convert, metamorphose

Read With the Best

NATHANIEL HAWTHORNE
– THE SCARLET LETTER (CHAPTERS 21-24)

WEEK 24

LITERARY ANALYSIS:

Didactic / Didacticism: Didacticism means the practice or art of providing instruction. In literature, this refers to the use of writing for teaching and offering moral, religious or ethical guidance. For an author's work to be didactic, his main purpose of writing must be to teach.

Denouement (Resolution or Falling Action): The final outcome of the plot of a play, novel, or other literary work. The denouement, resolution or falling action happens after the climax.

CRITICAL READING QUESTIONS:

1) What does the author say were the respectable qualities of eartly Puritan political leaders? *They were wise and had fortitude and self-reliance.*

2) What does Chillingworth do to interrupt Hester's and Dimmesdale's plan? *He buys a ticket to go on the same ship as them acting as the ship's doctor.*

3) What hypocrisy about the Puritans is displayed at the Procession? *Even though the Puritans are supposed to be plain and not worldly, the procession is pompous, loud, and is a display of power and opulence.*

4) What is the climax of this novel? *When Dimmesdale finally confesses his sin publicly and then dies*

5) What is the denouement, resolution, or falling action of this novel? (It can be more than one event or action.) *The denouement includes Chillingworth losing his chance for revenge and then dying, Pearl and Hester moving on and making lives for themselves, Pearl becoming human and living a normal life, etc.*

NATHANIEL HAWTHORNE
- The Scarlet Letter (Chapters 21-24)

WEEK 24

CRITICAL READING QUESTIONS (CONTINUED):

6) Why does Pearl finally become "human"?
She is given an earthly father for the first time.

7) How did many of the leaders respond to Dimmesdale's confession and revealing of his scarlet letter?
They denied seeing the "A" and said his sermon did not deal with Dimmesdale personally.

8) What is the main Theme of *The Scarlet Letter*? *Sin and hypocrisy*

9) In your own opinion, was Hawthorne's main purpose of writing *The Scarlet Letter* didactic?
Opinion; some authorities say Hawthorne's main purpose was narrative (or to tell a story) and not mainly didactic, but I believe he wrote it to teach about hypocrisy.

10) In your opinion, who is the victim of this novel? Why?
Answers will vary – Opinion

NATHANIEL HAWTHORNE
– THE SCARLET LETTER (CHAPTERS 21-24)

WEEK 24

MAKE IT REAL:

Think of at least two examples of literature we have read this year or other examples of literature that were clearly written for didactic purposes.
<u>Answers will vary. This year's literature can include</u> **<u>The Autobiography of Benjamin Franklin</u>** *<u>or</u>* **<u>A Narrative of the Captivity and Restoration of Mary Rowlandson</u>** *<u>or "Sinners in the Hands of an Angry God."</u>*

Nathaniel Hawthorne
– The Scarlet Letter (Chapters 21-24)

Week 24

WRITING ASSIGNMENT:

This week, you will write your thesis statement for your research paper and your title. Please note that we will write our title and thesis statement before we take notes. (This is different from the book.) In *Writing a Research Paper,* read pages 69-73 and complete Exercise 7 and odd numbers only for Exercise 8.

NATHANIEL HAWTHORNE
- THE SCARLET LETTER (CHAPTERS 21-24)

WEEK 24

CULMINATING ACTIVITY:

Pretend you are a television reporter assigned to report the Procession and Election Day events in Chapter 23. You witness the scene on the scaffold and must report it from your viewpoint right after Dimmesdale dies. In a group, have some members act out the scene and one person serve as the reporter.

Edgar Allan Poe
"The Raven", "Annabel Lee" & "Ligeia"
Week 25

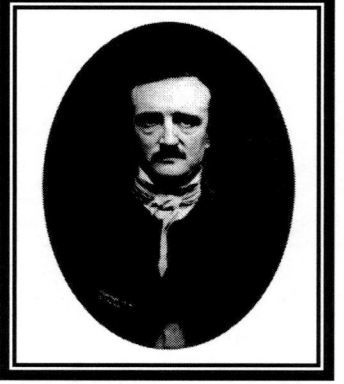

> *"On this home by Horror haunted*
> *- tell me truly, I implore -*
> *Is there - is there balm in Gilead?*
> *- tell me - tell me, I implore!*
> *Quoth the raven, 'Nevermore.'"*

Edgar Allan Poe

Background Check:

1) What happened to disillusion Poe and make him begin to miss classes at West Point Academy? **His foster father remarried and had a biological son that would inherit his fortune instead of Poe.**

2) Poe is often called "The Father" of what two literary genres? (You may have to research this.) **The modern short story/detective story; Gothic Horror**

3) Who did Poe marry, and how old was she? What happened to her? **Virginia Clemm, his cousin; she was 13; She died of tuberculosis very young.**

4) Why was Poe often fired from jobs? **He had a serious drinking problem.**

5) Was it Poe's ambition to become more of a poet or a literary critic? **Literary critic**

6) What was Poe's main purpose in writing poetry? **To appeal to the sense of beauty**

7) How old was Poe when he died? **40**

Edgar Allan Poe
"The Raven", "Annabel Lee" & "Ligeia"

Week 25

"The Raven" & "Annabel Lee"
Words To Know:

Identify the part of speech of each word, and give one or two synonyms for each.

lore	Noun	myth, traditional wisdom, adage, belief, doctrine, enlightenment, experience, fable
surcease	Verb	stop, defer, delay, desist, postpone, refrain, rest, stay
mien	Noun	manner, act, address, air, appearance, aspect, aura
obeisance	Noun	salutation, allegiance, bow, homage, honor, deference, loyalty, respect, reverence
placid	Adj.	calm, mild, collected, composed, detached, easygoing, peaceful
adjure	Verb	commend, beseech, charge, entreat, implore, order, require
pallid	Adj.	pale, dull, faded, ashen, feeble, ghastly, gray, lifeless, frail
seraphs	Noun	angels, guardians, spirits, holy beings
sepulchre	Noun	chambers, tombs, burial chambers
dissever	Verb	separate, cut, cut off, detach, divide, section, segment, sever, split, carve
dirges	Noun	laments, chants, cries, laments, hymns, requiems

Literary Analysis:

Denotation: The dictionary and literal meaning of a word

Connotation: The figurative or literary meaning of a word.

Example: The denotative meaning of "gold" is a metallic element. The connotative meaning is associated with riches, power, greed, and happiness.

Assonance: Repetition of vowel sounds in poetry, usually occurring in stressed syllables.

Example: "Twinkle, twinkle, little <u>star</u>, how I wonder what you <u>are</u>."

Edgar Allan Poe
– "The Raven", "Annabel Lee" & "Ligeia"

Week 25

"THE RAVEN" & "ANNABEL LEE"

CRITICAL READING QUESTIONS:

1) What point of view is "The Raven" written in? *First person*

2) In "The Raven", what was the narrator's dream that "no mortal ever dared to dream before"? *He dreamed his lover would come back from the dead.*

3) What did the narrator mean by the question, "Is there a balm in Gilead?"
He asked if there would ever be comfort (a balm) for his loss.

4) How does Poe create a melancholic mood in "The Raven"?
Developing the dreary and haunting setting, repetition of the word "nevermore", words such as "midnight" "weary", "bleak", "dying", "sorrow"

5) Cite some of the words or phrases Poe uses in "The Raven" in a connotative way.
"Fantastic", "my soul grew stronger", "ungainly", "balm"

6) What is the bird a symbol of in "The Raven"?
The narrator's never ending grief over the loss of his lover; death

7) In "Annabel Lee," why does the poet say the angels are envious of him and Annabel Lee? *The couple "loved with a love that was more than love."*

8) Cite an example of assonance in both poems.
-weak and weary
-lore, dore, more, floor, Lenore
-life, bride, nigh tide, bright eyes, rise

Read With the Best — Diagnostic Prescriptive Services | www.edudps.com

Edgar Allan Poe
– "The Raven", "Annabel Lee" & "Ligeia"

Week 25

"Ligeia"
Words To Know:

Identify the part of speech of each word, and give one or two synonyms for each.

Word	Part of Speech	Synonyms
cerements	Noun	coverings, cloaks, clothing, dresses, envelopes, garments
emaciated	Adj.	malnourished, undernourished, thin, starved, gaunt, haggard, lean
opium dream	Noun	an unrealistic expectation, a fantasy
rivaling	Verb	opposing, approaching, approximating, contending, corresponding, competing, matching
aquiline	Adj.	of, pertaining to, or a characteristic of an eagle; curved down like an eagle's beak
tumultuous	Adj.	confused, agitated, boisterous, clamorous, disturbed, excited, hectic
abstruse	Adj.	difficult to understand, abstract, complex, complicated, deep, enigmatic
erudition	Noun	higher education, cultivation, culture, enlightenment, knowledge
poignant	Adj.	affecting, painful, agonizing, bitter, distressing, emotional, disturbing, intense, moving, passionate
lambent	Adj.	luminous, bright, brilliant, glowing, lustrous, radiant
effulgence	Noun	brightness, blaze, brilliance, dazzle, luster, radiance, splendor
impetuously	Adj.	hastily, carelessly, foolishly, impulsively, rashly
dilate	Verb	stretch, widen, amplify, augment, broaden, develop, enlarge, expand, increase
imbibed	Verb	drunk, assimilated, consumed, downed, gorged
dotage	Noun	feebleness, old age, weakness, elderliness, infirmity
incipient	Adj.	basic, developing, beginning, elementary, fundamental, initial
phantasmagoric	Adj.	illusive, apparent, chimerical, deceitful, delusive, fallacious, fictitious, fanciful, illusory, imaginary, whimsical, untrue
pertinaciously	Adv.	with determination, constantly, intently, persistently, purposefully
pertinacity	Noun	obstinacy, determination, purpose, reluctance
waned	Verb	diminished, lessened, abated, declined, decreased, dropped, ebbed, faded, withered, subsided
livid	Adj.	pale, ashen, gloomy, lurid, pallid, wan, blanched

Edgar Allan Poe
- "The Raven", "Annabel Lee" & "Ligeia"

Week 25

"LIGEIA"
CRITICAL READING QUESTIONS:

1) What metaphors does Poe use to describe Ligeia's eyes?
"Divine orbs", "twin stars", "luminous orbs", "gazelle's eyes"

2) Where does the narrator meet Ligeia?
He can't remember at first, but then says, "In a city near the Rhine River..."

3) What point of view is this story written in? How does this affect the story?
First person; it makes the story more realistic, emotional, and suspenseful because the narrator experienced the events.

4) What drug was the narrator addicted to? *Opium*

5) What happens to Ligeia? *She dies.*

6) Why was the narrator's marriage to Rowena strained or not good?
He was obsessed with Ligeia and still loved her.

Why did he loathe Rowena? *Rowena did not love him.*

7) What is the major difference in the physical appearance of the narrator's two wives?
One has long black hair and dark eyes, and the other has blonde hair and blue eyes.

8) What did the narrator think he saw drop into the goblet of Rowena?
Drops of blood or red liquid

9) Who is alive at the end of the story? *Ligeia*
Why did she live? *She believed you die only if you will to die.*

Edgar Allan Poe
– "The Raven", "Annabel Lee" & "Ligeia"

Week 25

MAKE IT REAL:

Think of two words we use in modern language today. Write their denotative and connotative meanings.
Answers will vary.

Edgar Allan Poe
– "The Raven", "Annabel Lee" & "Ligeia"

Week 25

WRITING ASSIGNMENT:

(Make sure you have purchased large index cards with lines on them before taking notes next week.)

This week you will write a tentative outline for your research paper which you will use to help you take notes. You should write a topical outline. See *Write With The Best, Vol. 2* for help with writing an outline.

In *Writing a Research Paper,* read pages 47-48 and pages 50-62.

Read these pages carefully, and make sure you understand completely how to take notes and avoid plagiarism.

Complete exercises 4,5, and 11.

Edgar Allan Poe
- "The Raven", "Annabel Lee" & "Ligeia"

Week 25

CULMINATING ACTIVITY:

Alone or in a group, come up with the theme of "Ligeia" and the point that you think Poe is making in this story.

As a group activity, write a quick song, poem, commercial, or book review to present the theme to classmates.

Edgar Allan Poe
"The Fall of the House of Usher" & "The Purloined Letter"

Week 26

"Well, I may venture so far as to say that the paper gives its holder a certain power in a certain quarter where such power is immensely valuable."

Edgar Allan Poe

Literary Analysis:

Gothic Fiction or Horror: A style of fiction in literature characterized by gloomy settings, violent action or terror, a mood of decay or degeneration, and the supernatural.

Detective story: A story in which a mystery is revealed by a detective. Poe is recognized as the inventor of the detective story with his writing of "The Murder in The Rue Morgue". His favorite detective, Dupin, set the stage for Sherlock Holmes and other famous detectives.

Protagonist: The leading character of a literary work. The protagonist is not always the "hero," but is always the principal and central character.

Foil: A person or thing in a story that makes another person seem better or more prominent.

Edgar Allan Poe
"The Fall of the House of Usher" & "The Purloined Letter"

Week 26

"The Fall of the House of Usher"
Words To Know -

Identify the part of speech of each word, and give one or two synonyms for each.

affinity	Noun	affection, attraction, closeness, fondness
anomaly	Noun	aberration, departure, deviation, exception, incongruity, inconsistency
cadaverousness	Noun	pallor, paleness, bloodlessness, colorlessness
dank	Adj.	clammy, chilly, close, damp, humid, moist, slimy
distempered	Adj.	cluttered, disturbed, mixed up, bewildered, confused, angered, annoyed
gossamer	Adj.	gauzy, thin, airy, delicate, sheer, light, fine, flimsy, labyrinth, net, mesh, network
hypochondria	Noun	chronic and abnormal anxiety about imaginary symptoms and ailments
importunate	Adj.	demanding, insistent, burning, clamorous, disturbing, earnest
incubus	Noun	evil spirit, demon, devil, fiend, nightmare
interment	Noun	burial, burying, funeral, entombment, sepulture, obsequy
irrepressible	Adj.	effervescent, vivacious, boisterous, buoyant, ebullient, enthusiastic, rebellious
munificent	Adj.	giving, beneficent, generous, benevolent, bountiful, charitable, kind, lavish, liberal
protracted	Verb & Adj.	extended, drawn out, continued, delayed, prolonged, postponed
supposititious	Adj.	supposed, alleged, apparent, hypothetical, likely
cataleptic	Adj. / Noun	of or having characteristics of catalepsy (a nervous condition characterized by muscular rigidity) / a person suffering from catalepsy

Read With the Best

Edgar Allan Poe
"The Fall of the House of Usher" & "The Purloined Letter"

Week 26

"The Fall of the House of Usher"
Critical Reading Questions:

1) How did the narrator of this story know Roderick Usher?
The two were childhood friends.

2) What physical ailments did Usher have?
Nervousness and very acute, active senses

3) How do the opening lines establish the tone of this short story?
The author uses nouns, adjectives, and adverbs to create the tone – dull, dark, soundless, oppressively, dreary, melancholy, insufferable, gloom
What is this tone? *The tone is dark, gloomy, and melancholic.*

4) What do Usher's books reveal about his personality and state of mind?
He reads about the same things that haunt him – torture, mysticism, devils, journeys into the imagination, etc.

5) What does Roderick think will eventually kill him? *Fear*

6) What instrument does Usher play? *Guitar*

7) Why does Usher think the stones of the house are alive?
He can feel them watching him; they are possessed by his ancestors.

8) What is wrong physically with Usher's sister, Madeline?
She has occasional paralysis.
Why does Usher have such a close bond with her?
They are twins, and she is his last family.

Read With the Best

Edgar Allan Poe
– "The Fall of the House of Usher" & "The Purloined Letter"

WEEK 26

"The Fall of the House of Usher"
Critical Reading Questions (continued):

9) What elements of Romanticism do you see in this story?
This story emphasizes the supernatural, the imagination over reasoning, and the feelings and emotions of the characters.

10) Cite three examples from the story to prove this is Gothic fiction.
A gloomy setting (the house), the terror and frightening suspense, and the supernatural with Madeline and the house

11) What happens to Usher in the end? *Madeline kills him.*

Edgar Allan Poe
"The Fall of the House of Usher" & "The Purloined Letter"

Week 26

"The Purloined Letter"
Words To Know

Identify the part of speech of each word, and give one or two synonyms for each.

cant	Noun	deceit, hypocrisy, insincerity, pretense, dishonesty, show dialect, diction, idiom, language, slang
aufait	Adj.	to the point, fully informed, socially informed, fully competent
personage	Noun	celebrity, notable, chief, individual, luminary, eminence, being, notable
doggerel	Noun	poetry, expression, rhythmic literary work, balladry, rhyme, song
gimlet	Noun	drill, tool, implement, punch, bit
prodigious	Adj.	huge, enormous, fantastic, giant, gigantic, immense, monstrous, mighty, tremendous, shocking, awesome
escritoire	Noun	desk, davenport, secretary, case, wardrobe, repository
functionary	Noun	administrator, factor, intermediary, officer, minister, lawyer, advocate, ambassador, assistant
spurious	Adj.	counterfeit, fake, affected, artificial, contrived, deceitful, imitation, mock, phony
profundity	Noun	wisdom, acumen, balance, caution, discernment, enlightenment, information, insight, stability, understanding
ingenuity	Noun	ability, adroitness, brilliance, creativity, cunning, intelligence, genius, mastery, gift, expertise
acumen	Noun	awareness, comprehension, ingenuity, intellect, insight, perception
promulgate	Verb	make known, advertise, announce, broadcast, call, notify, proclaim
educed	Verb	brought out, elicited, concluded, deduced, derived, gained, got
egregious	Adj.	conspicuous, outstanding, exceptional
clandestinely	Adv.	secretly, scrumptiously, confidentially, stealthily
intriguant	Noun	one that intrigues
ruse	Noun	trick, deception, angle, artifice, device, gambit

Edgar Allan Poe
"The Fall of the House of Usher" & "The Purloined Letter"

WEEK 26

"The Purloined Letter"
Critical Reading Questions:

1) Who is the protagonist in this story? *Dupin*

2) How does Dupin successfully solve the mystery of this story? *By using logical deductive reasoning and his brains/ intelligence and thinking like the criminal thinks*

3) What kind of allusions does Poe use in this story? *Classical allusions*

4) What example of foreshadowing do you find early in the story to prepare you for the solving of the crime in the end? *The Prefect considered everything "odd"; the Prefect observed that Minister D. stayed away from his apartment many nights of the week.*

5) What is the tone of this story? *Light, jovial and a competitive tone between Dupin and the Prefect*

6) What specific point of view is the story written in? *First person limited point of view* Why do you think Poe uses this point of view? *Poe gives the narrator limited knowledge, so the readers are held in suspense until the end.*

7) What is the actual crime in this story? *Stealing an incriminating letter and using it for blackmail*

8) How does the Prefect display erroneous logic? *He assumes the minister would react like everyone else would and would hide the letter using methods everyone else would use.*

9) Is this story an example of Poe's Gothic fiction? *No*

10) Who is the foil in this story? *The Prefect*

Edgar Allan Poe
- "The Fall of the House of Usher" & "The Purloined Letter"

Week 26

MAKE IT REAL:

Think of two examples of foils in literature or movies.
Answers will vary.

Edgar Allan Poe
"The Fall of the House of Usher" & "The Purloined Letter"

Week 26

Writing Assignment:

This week you will be taking notes on your large note cards for your research paper. Do at least 3-4 cards. Make sure you closely follow the guidelines in your book, *Writing a Research Paper*, on pages 55 and 56.
Label each card with a topic from your outline, and make sure each card tells which source and the page numbers you are using.

_____

_____

_____

_____

_____

_____

_____

_____

_____

_____

_____

Culminating Activity:

Choose the protagonist from one of the five works of Poe you have read including his poetry. Alone, write out a talk show script in which you interview the protagonist.
In groups, have each group present the protagonist to the audience.
One person will be the host, and the protagonist and his friends or acquaintances will be the guests.
As a group, have the audience guess the protagonist you are presenting.

Herman Melville
– "Bartleby the Scrivener"

WEEK 27

Herman Melville

> "Will you tell me, Bartleby, where you were born?"
> "I would prefer not to."
> "Will you tell me anything about yourself?"
> "I would prefer not to."

Background Check:

1) Where was Melville born? **New York City**

2) How long did Melville go to formal school? **Until he was 12**

3) Which novel of Melville's has often been praised as the greatest novel in English? (Research this) **Moby Dick**

4) Which other famous American writer was Melville's friend? **Hawthorne**

5) Did Melville receive strong literary recognition at the end of his life? **No**

6) Which book of Melville's was published after his death? What was it about?
Billy Budd; a sailor who is wrongly accused and suffers wrong

7) How did Melville say he was like Shakespeare?
They both told the truth about man and life in their writings.

Herman Melville — "Bartleby the Scrivener"
Week 27

LITERARY ANALYSIS:

Antagonist: The chief opponent of the main character of a literary work. This can be a person or force.

WORDS TO KNOW:

Identify the part of speech of each word, and give one or two synonyms for each.

avocations	Noun	hobbies, amusements, diversions, occupations, pastimes, recreations
divers	Adj.	various, assorted, diverse, manifold, many, miscellaneous, sundry, varied
waive	Verb	give up, let go, abandon, allow, cede, delay, postpone, hand over, renounce, resign, surrender
remunerate	Verb	compensate, reward, accord, award, grant, pay, redress
abrogation	Noun	cancellation, ending, withdrawal, invalidation, discontinuation, annihilation
conferred	Verb	discussed, deliberated, advised, bargained, consulted, discoursed; allotted, accorded, bestowed, donated, gave approval, granted
averse	Adj.	afraid, opposing, afraid, agnostic, contrary, hostile, reluctant, unwilling
augmented	Verb	made greater, improved, aggrandized, amplified, built up, expanded, intensified, strengthened
eccentricities	Noun	bizarreness, unusualness, aberrations, caprices, quirks, idiosyncrasies
fervid	Adj.	passionate, ardent, impassioned, enthusiastic, burning, eager, fierce, passionate, zealous
usurpation	Noun	seizing something, apprehension, assumption, arrest, snatch, seizing
maledictions	Noun	anathemas, curses, damnations, abuses
reproach	Noun / Verb	strong criticism, dishonor, abuse, blame, condemnation, disgrace, shame, rebuke; find fault with, admonish, condemn, scold
obstreperousness	Noun	unruliness, assertiveness, imprudence, opposition, recklessness, wildness
insolent	Adj.	bold, disrespectful, arrogant, brazen, overbearing
insolence	Noun	boldness, disrespect, arrogance, contempt, impudence
paroxysms	Noun	seizures, spasms, agitations, attacks, fits, frenzies, rages, outbursts

Herman Melville
"Bartleby the Scrivener"
Week 27

WORDS TO KNOW (CONTINUED):

alacrity	Noun	liveliness, promptness, avidity, speed, readiness, zeal, agility
mollified	Verb	pacified, soothed, abated, allayed, appeased, calmed, relieved, softened, quieted
recondite	Adj.	mysterious, obscure, abstruse, arcane, difficult, mystical, profound, abstract
pallid	Adj.	pale, ashen, dull, faded, lifeless, weak, anemic, frail
pallidity	Noun	pallor, paleness, wanness, bloodlessness, whiteness
execrable	Adj.	horrible, sickening, abhorrent, abominable, horrific, loathsome, repulsive, vile, disgusting, detestable
imperative	Adj.	necessary, acute, burning, clamorous, important, obligatory, pressing
ignominiously	Adv.	disgracefully, embarrassingly, shamefully, despicably, contemptibly, vilely, meanly
dyspeptic	Adj.	crabby, irritable, mean, ornery, bad-tempered, disagreeable
invariable	Adj.	not changing, consistent, fixed, rigid, set, unchanging
vagary	Noun	caprice, fancy, humor, idea, impulse, notion, whim
inadvertently,	Adv.	carelessly, heedlessly, rashly, recklessly, accidentally, unintentionally
inadvertent	Adj.	accidental, careless, heedless, thoughtless, unintentional
imprudently	Adv	unwisely, foolishly, indiscreetly, rashly
incubus	Noun	evil spirit, demon, devil, fiend, nightmare

CRITICAL READING QUESTIONS:

1) What age is the narrator of this story? *Elderly*
   What is the narrator's profession? *Lawyer*

2) The narrator has always believed that the *easiest* way is the best way.

3) What is the setting of this story? *Wall St., New York City*

4) What is a scrivener? *A legal copyist*

HERMAN MELVILLE
– "BARTLEBY THE SCRIVENER"

WEEK 27

CRITICAL READING QUESTIONS (CONTINUED):

5) The narrator is perplexed by Bartleby's what? _Passivity or passive nature_

6) What statement does Bartleby often make when he doesn't want to do something? _"I prefer not to."_
What is the first time he makes this statement?
When he is asked to proofread copies for the narrator

7) What effect does Bartleby have on the narrator's and other scriveners' speech?
They all begin to say "prefer" without realizing it.

8) What important discovery does the narrator make about Bartleby once he finally accepts him? _Bartley lives at the law office_
What ends up being Bartleby's last home? _Prison_

9) Name at least 2 themes of this story.
Isolation, charity or compassion, world of work and business

10) How does the narrator finally fire or get rid of Bartleby?
He moves his office to another building.

11) Did Melville usually reveal the trait of optimism that most Transcendental authors portrayed? _No_
How do the closing lines of this story prove your answer to this question?
"Oh Bartleby, Oh humanity"; these show pessimism about humanism.

12) In your opinion, who is the antagonist in this story?
Opinion: Some would say the narrator is the antagonist because he opposed Bartleby in some ways and is in conflict with him. Some may even argue that Bartleby himself is his own worst enemy. He has no motivation or initiative and therefore lives a miserable life.

Herman Melville
– "Bartleby the Scrivener"

Week 27

Make It Real:

Think of three other antagonists in literary works we have read this year.
__Answers will vary, but may include: Roger Chillingworth, Rip Van Winkle's wife, and Pap from__ Huckleberry Finn.

Writing Assignment:

You will continue to take notes this week from the sources you have found for your research paper. Remember to follow the guidelines from *Writing A Research Paper*. Make sure you list the source, author, and page numbers on each card. This week, you should write at least 4-5 cards.

HERMAN MELVILLE
- "Bartleby the Scrivener"

WEEK 27

CULMINATING ACTIVITY:

Discuss whether you think Melville's method of pessimism in revealing the truth about man and life was as affective as a writer such as Hawthorne, who portrayed the cold hard facts but also left some hope at the end of his stories. As a group activity, create another ending to "Bartleby," and present it to the class.

Emily Dickinson
Poems 39, 112, 124, 202, 207, 236, 320, & 340
Week 28

> *"Success is counted sweetest*
> *By those who ne'er succeed.*
> *To comprehend a nectar*
> *Requires sorest need."*

Emily Dickinson

Background Check:

1) How did Emily Dickinson influence other writers?
She influenced the way they thought about poetic craft and vocation, and she was unique in her subject matter.

2) How many of Emily Dickinson's poems survived or were found? *1,800*

3) Was Dickinson recognized as a great poet in her lifetime? Why was she rejected by some publishers?
No; they could not accept her nontraditional and unconventional approach and thought her new techniques were flawed.

4) What kind of personal suffering did she experience that may have influenced her writing?
She never married, lost many romantic interests and close family members, and had health problems.

5) Although she attended a female seminary, did Dickinson hold to traditional Christian teaching?
No

Emily Dickinson
Poems 39, 112, 124, 202, 207, 236, 320, & 340

Week 28

Words To Know:

Identify the part of speech of each word, and give one or two synonyms for each.

sod	Noun	clod, grass, pasture, meadow, lawn, mead
firmaments	Noun	heavens, skies, vaults, empyreans
tankards	Noun	mugs, cans, cups, flagons, flasks
inebriate	Verb	exhilarate, stimulate, intoxicate, make drunk
bobolink	Noun	a migratory American songbird
chorister	Noun	chorus, ensemble, chorale, choir, group of singers
heft	Verb	carry, haul, lift, bear, sustain, take, pull, raise, boost, drag
imperial	Adj.	regal, domineering, majestic, royal, sovereign, administrative
debauchee	Noun	hedonist, libertine, deviant, pervert, a dissolute person
surplice	Noun	a long robe, angels

Literary Analysis:

Slant rhyme or Approximate rhyme: The substitution of assonance (words with the similar vowel sounds) for real rhyme.

Example: Giver and never

Enjambment: The running on of thought from one line, couplet (pair of lines), or stanza to the next.

EMILY DICKINSON
Poems 39, 112, 124, 202, 207, 236, 320, & 340

Week 28

CRITICAL READING QUESTIONS:

1) In Poem 39, what does the speaker imply she lost twice? *Two people she loved*

2) In Poem 39, who is she speaking to as "Burglar", "Banker" and "Father"? What could she mean by these names?
She is talking to God as a robber who took her loved ones away, a banker who can reimburse her with others to love and a father who can comfort her.

3) According to the speaker in Poem 112, who most values success?
Those who never succeed

4) What is the connotative meaning of "comprehend" in the third line of the first stanza of Poem 112? *Enjoy, appreciate*

5) Why does Dickinson capitalize words such as "Flag" and "Victory"?
For emphasis, to give higher meaning

6) Give an example of slant rhyme in Poem 112.
"Today" and "victory", "sweetest" and "succeed", "dying" and "triumph"

7) Whom is the poet referring to in stanza one of Poem 124? Where are they?
The dead; in their caskets, coffins, or burial boxes

8) In Poem 202, who are the gentlemen who can "see"?
Perhaps those who have eyes of faith to see things that can only be seen with faith or those who are close observers, or those who act on evidence

9) Who is the narrator of Poem 207? *A bird and probably a hummingbird; possibly a flower*

EMILY DICKINSON
Poems 39, 112, 124, 202, 207, 236, 320, & 340

Week 28

CRITICAL READING QUESTIONS (CONTINUED):

10) What is the tone of Poem 236? *Light, jovial, playful, informal, jubilant, happy*

11) When the narrator in Poem 236 says she just wears her "wings", what do "wings" refer to? *Birds*
Who is the little sexton? *A bird*

12) What is heaven to the narrator of Poem 236?
When she communes with nature or nature itself

13) In Poem 320, how are the shadows personified? What does this mean?
They hold their breath – things remain still and don't move, and everything stops.

14) In Poem 320, give two examples of enjambment.
"like the Heft, Of Cathedral Tunes –"
"But eternal difference, where the Meanings, are –"

15) What does the slant of light symbolize in Poem 320?
Grief, despair, heaviness, dread, sad memories

16) Which sense (sight, hearing, touch, taste, smell) does the imagery in Poem 340 appeal to most?
Sound/hearing

17) Give an example of slant rhyme in Poem 340. *Fro and through, down and then*

18) Whose funeral is the narrator talking about in Poem 340? *Her own*

19) What happens at the end of this poem?
The narrator dies or stops knowing or is buried.

EMILY DICKINSON
Poems 39, 112, 124, 202, 207, 236, 320, & 340

Week 28

MAKE IT REAL:

What other writers did we read this year that wrote about grief, despair, and death? In your opinion, did they do it with the same intensity as Emily Dickinson?

Anne Bradstreet
Edgar Allan Poe
Nathaniel Hawthorne

Opinion

_____
_____
_____
_____
_____
_____
_____
_____
_____
_____
_____
_____
_____
_____
_____
_____

Emily Dickinson
Poems 39, 112, 124, 202, 207, 236, 320, & 340

Week 28

WRITING ASSIGNMENT:

This is your last week to take notes for your research paper. Remember that your paper must be 5 pages typed, so you must have a great deal of information written in your notes in order to have a 5-page paper.

Remember that you should have only three long quotes, at the most, in your paper. You will need to paraphrase a lot of the information that you get from your research.

Emily Dickinson
Poems 39, 112, 124, 202, 207, 236, 320, & 340

Week 28

CULMINATING ACTIVITY:

Alone or as a group, pick one of the poems you read this week and paraphrase it in modern language.

Emily Dickinson
Poems 372, 409, 479, 591, 764, 1096, 1773

Week 29

*"Because I could not stop for Death–
He kindly stopped for me–
The carriage held but just Ourselves–
And Immortality."*

Emily Dickinson

Words To Know:

Identify the part of speech of each word, and give one or two synonyms for each.

ample	Adj.	fully sufficient, abundant, more than necessary, plenty, substantial
civility	Noun	niceness, compliance, courtesy, propriety
surmise	Noun / Verb	guess, conclusion, assumption, estimate, theory; assume, conclude, imagine, infer, speculate, suspect
interposed	Verb	interrupted, interceded, interfered, moderated, negotiated
cordial	Adj.	friendly, sociable, cheerful, happy, hearty, welcoming, tender, warm
cordiality	Noun	friendliness, sociability, sincerity, approval, understanding, warmth
vesuvian	Noun	a slow burning match formerly used for lighting cigars; a fuse

Emily Dickinson
Poems 372, 409, 479, 591, 764, 1096, 1773

Week 29

LITERARY ANALYSIS:

Quatrain: A stanza or poem of four lines. It is the most common English stanza form.

Ballad stanza: A stanza consisting of four lines rhyming abcb. Usually the first and third lines contain four accented syllables and the second and fourth contain three.

Consonance: A repetition of consonant sounds especially at the end of words.

Example: Discuss and dismiss.

CRITICAL READING QUESTIONS:

1) What is personified in Poem 372? **Nerves and the heart**

2) Why does Dickinson use dashes in her poetry?
To create a pause, continuance, suspense and to add more life, tension, feeling

3) What is the poet describing in Poem 372?
The recovering from or feeling after great pain or loss, grief, or dying

4) What is the soul compared to in Poem 409?
A noble lady or woman, queen, or person of royalty

5) "Close the valves of her own attention- Like Stone" means what?
The narrator makes her heart like stone toward those who want her attention, or she has lost interest and shut herself off emotionally.

6) In Poem 479, what kind of man is Death depicted as? **A gentleman**

7) How is Poem 479 in ballad stanza form?
It has rhymes on the 2nd and 4th lines of quatrains mainly and the accented syllables. There is some slant rhyme also.

Read With the Best | Diagnostic Prescriptive Services | www.edudps.com

Emily Dickinson
Poems 372, 409, 479, 591, 764, 1096, 1773
Week 29

CRITICAL READING QUESTIONS (CONTINUED):

8) The process of dying is depicted as what metaphor in Poem 479?
A carriage ride

9) Does the speaker of Poem 591 portray the final moments before her death as hysterically as many poets portray death?
No – she portrays it as peaceful.

10) What example of synecdoche do you see in Poem 591?
Eyes and breaths

11) What could the dash at the very end of the poem indicate?
That perhaps the speaker died while in the middle of speaking

12) What is the major metaphor or conceit in Poem 764?
The speaker's life is compared to a loaded gun.

13) Give examples of consonance in Poem 1096. *Grass, rides, is*
How do these sounds relate to a snake? *they make a hissing sound.*

14) In Poem 1773, what might the speaker mean by her life "closing twice"?
She lost those she loved twice.

15) How can "parting" be all we know of heaven and all we need of hell?
Death is a promise of heaven and can also bring hell to those who lose someone.

EMILY DICKINSON
Poems 372, 409, 479, 591, 764, 1096, 1773

Week 29

MAKE IT REAL:

Think of two more examples of quatrains with ballad stanzas.
(Hint: Think of nursery rhymes or songs.)
"Mary Had a Little Lamb"
"Jack Be Nimble"
"Little Bo Peep"

Emily Dickinson
- Poems 372, 409, 479, 591, 764, 1096, 1773

Week 29

WRITING ASSIGNMENT:

Look carefully at all the notes you have taken for your research paper. Revise your outline as necessary. Your new outline will serve as a guide as you begin to write your rough draft. It does not have to be perfect. You will finalize it later. Read pages 88-92 in *Writing a Research Paper*.

Write the rough draft of your introduction only this week. Make sure you cite the authors and page numbers of where you got your words and ideas. Refer to pages 109-114 in *Writing a Research Paper* for help with this. Your introduction should not have many citations.

Emily Dickinson
Poems 372, 409, 479, 591, 764, 1096, 1773

Week 29

CULMINATING ACTIVITY:

Alone, try to draw illustrations for Poem 479.
As a group activity, have one person or more read the poem while the rest of the group pantomimes it or acts it out. Use creativity and visual aids if possible.

Henry David Thoreau
"Resistance to Civil Government" or "Civil Disobedience"

Week 30

"A man has not every thing to do, but something; and because he cannot do everything, it is not necessary that he should do something wrong."

Henry David Thoreau

BACKGROUND CHECK:

1) Why did Thoreau's parents choose to send him to Harvard instead of his other siblings? <u>He showed academic promise at an early age (memorizing Shakespeare at age 10), and they could only afford to send one.</u>

2) Who was a famous student of Thoreau's at his school? <u>Louisa May Alcott</u>

3) Who was the most important influence and friend in the life of Thoreau? <u>Ralph Waldo Emerson</u>

4) What incident in Thoreau's life inspired his essay "Resistance to Civil Government"? <u>Being jailed for not paying his poll tax because he thought the Mexican War was proslavery</u>

5) What main cause did Thoreau take up in the 1850's, and what infamous person did he fully support? <u>Abolitionism/ antislavery; John Brown</u>

6) What two famous world figures were inspired by Thoreau's essay "Resistance to Civil Government"? <u>Ghandi and Martin Luther King, Jr.</u>

Read With the Best — Diagnostic Prescriptive Services | www.edudps.com

Henry David Thoreau
"Resistance to Civil Government" or "Civil Disobedience"

WEEK 30

WORDS TO KNOW:

Identify the part of speech of each word, and give one or two synonyms for each.

gregariousness	Noun	friendship, fellowship, companionship, intimacy, togetherness
requisitions	Noun	appeals, questions, recourses, pleas, petitions, entreaties
unconciliatory	Adj.	not agreeable
indispensablest	Adj.	most essential
impetuous	Adj.	acting without thinking, abrupt, hasty, impulsive, sudden, rash
foist	Verb	force upon, oppose, compel to accept, insert fraudulently
prudence	Noun	caution, head, care, tact, vigilance, foresight, diligence, sense, restraint
behoves	Verb	befits, is necessary or proper
inexpedient	Adj.	futile, detrimental, imprudent
alacrity	Noun	liveliness, promptness, avidity, enthusiasm, zeal, readiness
unscrupulous	Adj.	immoral, base, deceitful, dishonest, petty, shady, scandalous, sly, unfair
expedient (noun)	Noun	resource, device, method, medium, stratagem, means
diabolical	Adj.	devilish, cruel, evil, heinous, vicious, vile, wicked

Use three of these words in a sentence about a citizen resisting the government. ***Answers will vary.***

_____

_____

_____

LITERARY ANALYSIS:

Antithesis: The placement of sharply contrasting and contradictory ideas in parallel or balanced words, phrases, or ideas.

Examples are: "To err is human, to forgive divine" and "Man proposes, God disposes."

Henry David Thoreau
"Resistance to Civil Government" or "Civil Disobedience"

Week 30

CRITICAL READING QUESTIONS:

1) What rhetorical device does Thoreau use at the beginning of Paragraph 4 of this essay? _Rhetorical questions_

2) Thoreau states that it is not the government that achieves the things that it has been credited with, but the _character_ of the American people.

3) What two current injustices does Thoreau speak against in the essay?
The invasion of Mexico and enslavement of one sixth of the population

4) Thoreau argues that the main opponents of reform and change are whom?
Those who do nothing and passively tolerate the status quo or who passively wait for others to create change; specifically merchants and farmers

5) Does Thoreau believe that voting is the proper solution to the government's injustices?
_No_
If not, what is? _Protesting/action_
Who wins in voting? _The majority_

6) What was Thoreau's primary act of civil disobedience in his own life?
Refusal to pay taxes

7) Why did Thoreau say man had a "right" to rebel against one's government?
Government is always evil.

8) What does Thoreau say a person should do concerning injustice?
Refuse to support something that is wrong

HENRY DAVID THOREAU
"RESISTANCE TO CIVIL GOVERNMENT" OR "CIVIL DISOBEDIENCE"

CRITICAL READING QUESTIONS (CONTINUED):

9) Which does Thoreau put more emphasis on – being a citizen or an individual?
An individual

10) What kind of people does Thoreau say are rare in the world's history and have not appeared yet in America?
Those with legislative genius

11) What metaphor does Thoreau use to describe the government? *A machine*

12) Find an example of antithesis in the middle of Thoreau's essay (around the 19th paragraph).
"A man has not everything to do, but something."
"…because he cannot do everything, it is not necessary that he should do some thing wrong."
"Government is best which governs not at all."

HENRY DAVID THOREAU
"Resistance to Civil Government" or "Civil Disobedience"

WEEK 30

MAKE IT REAL:

Name two specific ways that this essay could have influenced the actions of Gandhi and Martin Luther King.
Both Ghandi and M. L. King, Jr. fought against unjust laws for the sake of others.

WRITING ASSIGNMENT:

You will finish the rough draft of your research paper this week, including the body of your paper and your conclusion. Read pages 94-106 in *Writing a Research Paper* carefully.

After writing your rough draft, proofread it carefully.

Henry David Thoreau
"Resistance to Civil Government" or "Civil Disobedience"

Week 30

CULMINATING ACTIVITY:

As a group, take Thoreau's position on government and have someone else take the opposite position. Have each side make at least 3 valid points. Use examples from Thoreau's essay.

As an individual, write 3 valid points for each side using examples from the essay.

Henry David Thoreau
- *Walden* (Chapter 1)

Week 31

HENRY DAVID THOREAU

"I went to the woods because I wished to live deliberately, to front only the essentials facts of life, and see if I could not learn what it had to teach, and not, when I came to die, discover that I had not lived."

Literary Analysis:

Hyperbole: An extreme exaggeration or overstatement used to make a point in literature.

Example: "I am so hungry I could eat a horse."

Words To Know:

Identify the part of speech of each word, and give one or two synonyms for each.

Word	Part of Speech	Synonyms
factitious	Adj.	unnatural, artificial, false, sham, counterfeit
tedium	Noun	dullness, monotony, boredom, ennui, routine, disinterest, weariness
palatable	Adj.	delicious, agreeable, acceptable, enjoyable, pleasant, satisfactory
cashier (v)	Verb	discard, expel, bounce, discharge, dismiss, remove, terminate
apotheosize	Verb	exalt, aggrandize, glorify, elevate, idolize, laud, worship
caviler	Noun	critic, carper, faultfinder, nitpicker, quibbler, whiner
abstemiousness	Noun	sobriety, abstinence, restraint, ascetic
garret	Noun	attic, loft, turret, watchtower, cockloft
umbrageous	Adj.	filled with shade, cloudy, indistinct, dim, sheltered
philanthropy	Noun	humanitarianism, altruism, assistance, charity, fund, donation, generosity, relief
beneficence	Noun	donation, aid, goodness, generosity, goodness, kindness, charity
indispensable	Adj.	necessary, basic, crucial, required, vital, imperative, key, fundamental
defrauding	Verb / Adj.	cheating, bilking, bamboozling, deluding, swindling
obscurities	Noun	vagueness, ambiguities, darkness, uncertainties
magnanimity	Noun	generosity, chivalry, philanthropy, altruism
enervates	Verb	tires, wears out, debilitates, exhausts, fatigues, weakens

Henry David Thoreau
- WALDEN (CHAPTER 1)

WEEK 31

CRITICAL READING QUESTIONS:

1) Why did Thoreau say he chose to talk mainly about himself and not others?
He did not know anybody as much as he knew himself.

2) According to Thoreau, why do men fail to enjoy the nature that surrounds them?
They are too preoccupied with mundane things and the chaos of life.

3) What does Thoreau say is the purpose of his "experiment"?
To show the benefits of a simplified lifestyle and to teach his fellow man

4) What are the four necessities of life according to Thoreau?
Food, shelter, clothing, fuel

How can these be easily obtained? *From nature*

5) How long did Thoreau's experiment last? *Two years, two months, two days*

6) Which does Thoreau say is better- to increase one's means to get necessities or to decrease one's needs?
To decrease one's needs

Read With the Best

Henry David Thoreau
- *Walden* (Chapter 1)

WEEK 31

CRITICAL READING QUESTIONS (CONTINUED):

7) What is significant about July 4, 1845, which is the day Thoreau moves into the house he built?
It is the day of his own independence from social norms, demands, and conventions.

8) What does Thoreau mean by "Most men live lives of quiet desperation"? Do you agree with this statement?
Most men just live day by day and survive, but are not really happy; opinion

9) According to Thoreau, what is the only kind of charity that will "hide a multitude of sins"?
One of which he is in unconscious and one that is constant and abundant; philanthropy

10) Who were the two gazers that Thoreau encouraged to look in his windows?
The sun and moon

11) Find an example of hyperbole in Chapter one.
"My life was so simple, I could live on nails."
"To save the universe from annihilation"
"We have adopted Christianity merely as an improvement of agriculture."

Henry David Thoreau
– *Walden* (Chapter 1)

Week 31

MAKE IT REAL:

Why do you think *Walden* is considered an important work of American literature? *<u>Because of its revolutionary ideas about society; Thoreau uses Nature and his experiment with Nature to write a didactic literary masterpiece full of imagery and other figurative language.</u>*

Think of other literary or real-life "experiences" like Thoreau's.
- <u>Frankenstein</u>
- <u>The Great American Experiment</u>
- <u>Into the Wild</u>
- <u>See You In 100 Years</u>

Henry David Thoreau
– *Walden* (Chapter 1)

Week 31

WRITING ASSIGNMENT:

This week you will type your paper, including your outline and bibliography page. See the guidelines for proofreading your paper in *Writing a Research Paper* on pages 122-137. Read through these pages before you start typing to make sure your paper is ready to be typed. Pages 152-153 will tell you exactly how to type your paper, and pages 154-159 give an example of a research paper. Complete Exercise 3 on page 117 before typing your bibliography page. Read pages 118-119 to help you type the bibliography page.

Henry David Thoreau
- *Walden* (Chapter 1)

Week 31

CULMINATING ACTIVITY:

Alone or in a group, create a short episode of "Survivor – Walden Style: The Introduction." In this introduction, present how you will conduct the survivor experiment and what you will use to conduct it. Next week, you will conclude your episode. In a group setting, orally or dramatically present this to your class.

Henry David Thoreau
– Walden (Chapters 2, 5, 17, & 18)

Week 32

Henry David Thoreau

> *"Most men live lives of quiet desperation."*

Words To Know:

Identify the part of speech of each word, and give one or two synonyms for each.

Word	Part of Speech	Synonyms
chanticleer	Noun	cock, rooster, chicken
auroral	Adj.	bright, brilliant, blazing, alight, illuminated, sparkling, radiant, shiny
somnolence	Noun	coma, deep unconsciousness, slumber, stupor, oblivion, lethargy
undulation	Noun	wave, fluctuation, roll, sway, surge, swell, throbbing, pulse, rhythm, pressure
founder	Noun	person who establishes an institution, architect, author, designer, generator, patron
perturbation	Noun	distress, anxiety, confusion, disorder, disturbance
alluvion	Noun	flood, cascade, deluge, torrent, gush. affliction, calamity, disaster, affliction, trial, wreck
cleaver	Noun	cutting instrument, foe, river, knife, axe, hatchet. burr, thorny bush, prick, nettle, spray, brier
clout	Noun	power, authority, influence, standing, weight, sway
repose	Noun / Verb	calm, rest, ease, respite, peace, quiet / relax, recline, place, stretch, settle, lounge
dissipating	Verb	expending, spending, consuming, depleting, lavishing, squandering, dispelling, dispersing, scattering, spreading, vanishing, disappearing, dissolving
insular	Adj.	narrow minded, closed, confined, detached, cut off, limited, restricted, separated
paltry	Adj.	poor, worthless, base, cheap, meager, insignificant, limited
supernumerary	Adj.	excessive, additional, extra, superfluous
requiem	Noun	hymn, mass, chant, eulogy, worship, dirge, cry, lament, march

Henry David Thoreau
– Walden (Chapters 2, 5, 17, & 18)

Week 32

LITERARY ANALYSIS:

Motif: a recurring feature such as a name, object, image, or phrase in a work of literature that contributes to the theme in some way.

CRITICAL READING QUESTIONS:

1) What did Thoreau consider a religious exercise that he did every morning?
Bathing in the pond

2) What time or period of the day was symbolic to Thoreau? What did it symbolize to him? *The morning; it symbolized the dawn and newness to him.*

3) Find at least 2 metaphors that Thoreau uses. (See Chapter 4)
"Time is but the stream I go a-fishing in", "My serenity is rippled, but not ruffled", "My hoe is Mt. Olympus."

4) Did Thoreau believe that the chief purpose of man is to "glorify God and enjoy him forever"? *No* Can we glean any truths from Thoreau's writings?
opinion

5) "Our life is frittered by detail…simplicity, simplicity, simplicity! Instead of three meals a day, eat one." Do you agree or disagree with Thoreau's statement? Do you think our culture and lives are too complicated?
Opinion

HENRY DAVID THOREAU
– WALDEN (CHAPTERS 2, 5, 17, & 18)

WEEK 32

CRITICAL READING QUESTIONS (CONTINUED):

6) What does Poe mean by the metaphor "suck all the marrow out of life"?
Live life to its fullest.

7) According to Thoreau, how can one avoid "black melancholy"?
Live in the midst of Nature and have your senses still.

8) What type of figurative language does Thoreau use constantly to make his point and describe life, Nature, and aspects of both? *Personification or metaphors*

9) According to Thoreau, what is a "Realometer"?
A means of measuring the reality of things

10) What does Thoreau value over love, money, or fame? *Truth*

11) Why do you think Thoreau ends *Walden* and leaves Walden Pond in the spring?
Opinion, but should state something about pointing others to renewal of their lives, the future, and their potential

12) "I went to the woods because I wished to live deliberately, to front only the essential facts of life, and see if I could not learn what it had to teach, and not, when I came to die, discover that I had not lived." Do you think Thoreau's experiment was successful? Why or why not?
Opinion

13) Name one motif in these chapters that helps develop the theme of Walden.
The seasonal cycle or different seasons

Henry David Thoreau
- Walden (Chapters 2, 5, 17, & 18)

Week 32

MAKE IT REAL:

Now that you have finished *Walden*, decide whether you think it can be classified as a sermon, a philosophical discourse, or a journal entry about a man's experiment in the woods.
Try to think of similar writings.
Opinion

_____

_____

_____

_____

_____

_____

_____

_____

_____

_____

_____

_____

_____

_____

_____

_____

_____

Henry David Thoreau
- Walden (Chapters 2, 5, 17, & 18)

Week 32

WRITING ASSIGNMENT:

This week you will finally complete your research paper by proofreading it and making necessary revisions. See tips in your book *Writing a Research Paper* on pages 122-148. Check carefully for any signs of plagiarism.
Complete the exercises if you feel you need extra practice with these skills. Use the checklist on the next page to grade your research paper.

Henry David Thoreau
– Walden (Chapters 2, 5, 17, & 18)

Week 32

CULMINATING ACTIVITY:

This week you will conclude "Survivor: Walden Style." Use everything you have read to give a presentation (in writing or orally in a group) of Thoreau's methods of surviving at Walden Pond.

FREDERICK DOUGLASS
NARRATIVE OF THE LIFE OF FREDERICK DOUGLASS (CHAPTERS I-IX)

WEEK 33

FREDERICK DOUGLASS

"The silver trump of freedom had roused my soul to eternal wakefulness. It was heard in every sound, and seen in every thing. It was ever present to torment me with a sense of my wretched condition... It looked from every star, it smiled in every calm, breathed in every wind, and moved in every storm."

BACKGROUND CHECK:

1) How long did Douglass fight for freedom by writing, lecturing, and involving himself in political activity? *50 years*

2) What was Douglass known as at the time of his death?
The most influential African American leader of the nineteenth century and one of the best orators of that time

3) Was Frederick Douglass the name he was born with?
No; He changed his name when he escaped.

4) What were two profound and unusual facts about the *Narrative* that Douglass wrote?
It was a national best seller that he wrote all by himself in his own words, and he was African American.

5) Why was Douglass forced to flee to Canada and England in 1859?
He was accused of conspiring with John Brown.

6) Where did his last speech take place? *At a women's rights rally*

7) Douglass was a champion of *human rights.*

Frederick Douglass
Narrative of the Life of Frederick Douglass (Chapters I-IX) — Week 33

Words To Know:

Identify the part of speech of each word, and give one or two synonyms for each.

odiousness	Noun	ugliness, nefariousness, monstrousness, unpleasantness
reposed	Verb	relaxed, reclined, lounged, deposited, slumbered, slept, stretched
ineffable	Adj.	too good for words, celestial, divine, holy, sacred, transcendent, ethereal, delightful, pleasing, satisfying
obdurate	Adj.	pigheaded, stubborn, callous, obstinate, rigid, unemotional, unrelenting, tough, perverse, adamant
sundered	Verb	separated, severed, broke, parted, split, disconnected
imbibe	Verb	to drink heavily, absorb, assimilate, down, gorge, partake, swallow, get drunk, guzzle
execrate	Verb	hate, abhor, curse, damn, denounce, detest, despise, loathe, vilify
impudence	Noun	audacity, insolence, gall, chutzpah
consummate	Adj.	ultimate, best, absolute, accomplished, complete, supreme, talented, gifted, ideal, whole, utter achieve, finish, carry, close, terminate, end
odium	Noun	shame, dishonor, abhorrence, antipathy, malice, rebuke, discredit
offal	Noun	garbage, debris, junk, waste, remains, trash
impudent	Adj.	bold, shameless, audacious, rude, cool, brazen, impertinent, insolent
chattel	Noun	property, capital, effects, gear, goods, slave, belongings
sunder	Verb	break, divide, part, undo, slice, split, detach, disconnect
profligate	Adj.	immoral, corrupt, abandoned, degenerate, vicious, wicked, wanton, lewd, loose, depraved, wasteful, extravagant, lavish, reckless, prodigal
dissipation	Noun	amusement, entertainment, binge, distraction, celebration, diversion, recreation, party, wantonness, debauchery, dissolution, waste, indulgence, disappearance, dissemination, distribution, spread
emancipate	Verb	set free, liberate, loose, deliver, discharge, release
sagacity	Noun	wisdom, acumen, comprehension, discernment, enlightenment, experience, intelligence, insight, knowledge, prudence, sense
pernicious	Adj.	bad, hurtful, baleful, dangerous, deadly, harmful

FREDERICK DOUGLASS
NARRATIVE OF THE LIFE OF FREDERICK DOUGLASS (CHAPTERS I-IX)

WEEK 33

LITERARY ANALYSIS:

Chiasmus: A figure of speech wherein the order of the words in the first half of a parallel clause are reversed in the second half.

Example: "He calls me but a fool. A fool, perhaps I am."

CRITICAL READING QUESTIONS:

1) What was the custom with baby slaves and their mothers? *They were taken away from their mothers at a young age so that they could never bond with them.*

2) Why did Douglass never remember seeing his mother in the light? *She only came to him in the middle of the night when no one could see her.*

3) Why did Douglass say slavery in the South would soon become unscriptural? *Ham was supposedly cursed because he was black; many slaves were no longer totally black, so that argument could no longer hold.*

4) What metaphor did Douglass use to describe slavery in the first chapters? *Hell* What was the bloodstained gate into this? *the beating of his aunt that he had to witness first hand*

5) What was the bed of most slaves? *The floor*

6) What did Douglass associate the songs of slaves with? *Misery and unhappiness*

7) What duties were assigned to Douglass on Colonel Loyd's plantation before the age of 7? *Running errands, driving cows, cleaning front yard, helping find birds shot down*

8) What 2 things did he suffer from most? *Hunger and cold*

FREDERICK DOUGLASS
Narrative of the Life of Frederick Douglass (Chapters I-IX)

WEEK 33

CRITICAL READING QUESTIONS (CONTINUED):

9) What did he eat as a child? *Mush*

10) Find an example of chiasmus at the beginning of Chapter 4 (IV).
"He was just a man for such a place, and it was just the place for such a man."

11) What did Douglass never give up even in the darkest times of slavery?
Hope and faith

12) Find an example of antithesis in Chapter 6. *"What he most dreaded, I most desired."*

13) Which two people does Douglass give credit for his learning to read?
Master and Mistress Auld
Did they both want him to read? *No*

14) What did Douglass say was the "first plain manifestation of that kind of Providence which has ever since attended me"? *Moving to Baltimore*

15) Give an example of personification of slavery in Chapter V (5).
"That slavery will not always be able to hold me in its foul embrace"

16) Who were Douglass' true reading teachers?
The white boys he met on the streets and his desire and determination

17) Why was it "an unpardonable offense to teach slaves to read in a Christian country"?
Because knowledge would free them and they would become discontented

FREDERICK DOUGLASS
NARRATIVE OF THE LIFE OF FREDERICK DOUGLASS (CHAPTERS I-IX)

WEEK 33

CRITICAL READING QUESTIONS (CONTINUED):

18) Why did Douglass sometimes feel that learning to read was more of a curse than a blessing? _Reading allowed him to see what he was missing._

19) What kept Douglass from taking his own life or the life of another? _His thirst for freedom_

20) What was regarded as the "most affricated development of meanness" even among slaveholders? _Letting a slave go hungry or not giving him enough to eat_
Did Master Thomas participate in this? _yes_

21) Douglass said that he did not know of one single _noble_ _act_ performed by his Master Thomas.

22) How did Master Thomas' conversion at the Methodist Camp meeting change him? _He became more harsh and mean._

23) Why did Douglass not mind going to live with Mr. Covey? _He would get enough to eat._

FREDERICK DOUGLASS
NARRATIVE OF THE LIFE OF FREDERICK DOUGLASS (CHAPTERS I-IX)

WEEK 33

MAKE IT REAL:

Think of other written or filmed accounts of slaves.
How do they compare to Douglass' writing and the effect of his writing on his audience?
Answers will vary.

FREDERICK DOUGLASS
NARRATIVE OF THE LIFE OF FREDERICK DOUGLASS (CHAPTERS I-IX)

WEEK 33

WRITING ASSIGNMENT:

This week you will plan your final essay for the year.

You will be comparing and contrasting two of the works we have read this year. You may choose any two works/authors and any one of the following to compare and contrast:
- Theme of works
- Writing style of authors
- Rhetorical devices of authors / argumentation and persuasiveness
- Tone
- Characters and characterization
- Figurative language and literary devices

You will plan your essay this week and write it next week. Compose a brief outline this week.

FREDERICK DOUGLASS
NARRATIVE OF THE LIFE OF FREDERICK DOUGLASS (CHAPTERS I-IX)

WEEK 33

CULMINATING ACTIVITY:

Some critics have described Douglass' narrative as a "novel written as an autobiography."
Alone or in groups, do a dramatic presentation, song, or poem on one of the novel components of his narrative. These include theme, characters (antagonist, protagonist), conflict, rising action, and setting.

_____

_____

_____

_____

_____

_____

_____

_____

_____

_____

_____

_____

_____

_____

_____

_____

_____

_____

FREDERICK DOUGLASS
Narrative of the Life of Frederick Douglass (Chapter X - Appendix)

WEEK 34

> "...for, between the Christianity of this land, and the Christianity of Christ, I recognize the widest possible difference... I love the pure, peaceable, and impartial Christianity of Christ: I therefore hate the cradle-plundering, partial and hypocritical Christianity of this land."
>
> FREDERICK DOUGLASS

Words To Know:

Identify the part of speech of each word, and give one or two synonyms for each.

Word	Part of Speech	Synonyms
trifle	Verb	toy with, mess around, flirt, fool, misuse, squander, lounge, idle, waste
elasticity	Noun	stretchiness, flexibility, resilience, fluidity, buoyant, frisky, resilient, taunt
goaded	Verb	egged on, incited, animated, aroused, bullied, instigated, provoked, stimulated, propelled, triggered
quailed	Verb	covered, shrunk, cringed, dropped, shuddered, recoiled, trembled
impudence	Noun	audacity, chutzpah, gall, insolence, confidence, assurance, courage, nerve, poise
imprudent	Adj.	brash, careless, foolish, heedless, inconsiderate, reckless, rash
imbue	Verb	infuse, saturate, diffuse, inculcate, instill, invest, sleep, pervade
feasible	Adj.	possible, doable, appropriate, beneficial, expedient, practical, viable, suitable, worthwhile
perdition	Noun	hell, abyss, affliction, condemnation, inferno, suffering, punishment, ruin, damnation
hectoring	Verb	bullying, badgering, baiting, dominating, nagging, irritating, tormenting, intimidating, teasing
redress	Noun	help, compensation, aid, amendment, assistance, payment, justice, reward, return, vengeance
interposed	Verb Adj.	interrupted, inserted, introduced, interfered, mediated, negotiated, moderated
imputations	Noun	ascriptions, accusations, allegations, attributions, insinuations
exculpate	Verb	forgive, absolve, clear, condone, excuse, pardon, vindicate, release, remit
habiliments	Noun	clothing, attire, apparel, clothes, dress, gowns, garbs

Read With the Best

FREDERICK DOUGLASS
- *NARRATIVE OF THE LIFE OF FREDERICK DOUGLASS* (CHAPTER X-APPENDIX)

WEEK 34

LITERARY ANALYSIS:

Parody: A humorous and satirical writing (poem, prose, or drama) that ridicules a person, event, situation, or serious work of literature.

CRITICAL READING QUESTIONS:

1) How was Mr. Covey a deceiver?
He deceived himself into believing he was a Christian and devout, even though he was very evil.

2) Why did Mr. Covey buy the slave woman Caroline?
To breed her to create more slaves

3) Find an example of parallelism in Chapter 10.
Answers will vary, but may include: "...I resolved for the first time, to go to my master, enter a complaint, and ask his protection."

4) What event was a turning point in Douglass' life that made him to be a slave in "form" but never again in "fact"? *Winning the fight with Mr. Covey*

5) What kind of slave holders did Douglass say were the worst?
Religious slaveholders

6) What did the ships symbolize for Douglass? *Freedom*

7) In Chapter X, (towards the end, around the 25th paragraph) Douglass personifies slavery and freedom. Name some characteristics of each. Who was standing on the side of each?
Slavery – glared frightfully, robes stained with blood, feasting upon our flesh; Freedom – half frozen, beckoning us to come; Grim Death

FREDERICK DOUGLASS
- NARRATIVE OF THE LIFE OF FREDERICK DOUGLASS (CHAPTER X-APPENDIX)

WEEK 34

CRITICAL READING QUESTIONS (CONTINUED):

8) What did Douglass tell Henry to do with his pass? *Eat it with his biscuit*

9) What was Douglass' motto when he finally escaped from slavery? *"Trust no man."*

10) Douglass stated that the slaveholders felt that "To make a contented slave, you must make a *thoughtless* one."

11) How did the North end up looking totally different than what Douglass expected?
It was beautiful and wealthy; he thought it would be very poor because there were no slaves.
What was shocking about the free slaves in New York?
They weren't poor and were intelligent and well-read.

12) Why does Douglass write the Appendix to his narrative?
To let his readers know he was not an opponent of all religion

13) What Biblical group does Douglass compare to the slave holders and slave masters of his time? *The Pharisees*

14) Name at least 4 specific examples of blatant hypocrisy in cruel slave holders.
Answers will vary, but may include:
1) Ministers who claim to be ministers of the meek and lowly Jesus beat slaves during the week.
2) Douglass' Sunday School teacher who teaches him the way of salvation and then robs him of his earnings at the end of each week.
3) He who sells his sister for prostitution stands forth as an advocate of purity.
4) Slaveholders use the money they have made on slaves to support the church.

FREDERICK DOUGLASS
NARRATIVE OF THE LIFE OF FREDERICK DOUGLASS (CHAPTER X-APPENDIX)

CRITICAL READING QUESTIONS (CONTINUED):

15) Did Douglass believe the religion of America was Christianity? *No*

16) Why do you think Douglass remained a believer and follower of Jesus Christ despite his immense suffering?
Opinion, but may include: he had true faith in the goodness and faithfulness of God, and he believed in the truth of the Bible.

17) What is the main point of the parody Douglass includes in the appendix?
To ridicule the hypocrisy and cruelty of slaveholders

18) There are several themes in Douglass' narratives. List at least three of these.
A) Knowledge is power
B) Freedom
C) Hypocrisy (hypocritical professing Christians)
D) God's providence

FREDERICK DOUGLASS
NARRATIVE OF THE LIFE OF FREDERICK DOUGLASS (CHAPTER X-APPENDIX)

WEEK 34

MAKE IT REAL:

You are to list all the examples of figurative language or literary analysis terms we have learned this year that you find in your reading of Frederick Douglass' narrative (Hint: There are at least 20 examples.) How does Douglass' use of these improve the quality of his writing?

Apostrophe	*Tone*	*Crisis*
Anaphora	*Allusion*	*Style*
Antithesis	*Climax*	*Prose*
Chiasmus	*Irony*	*Parody*
Imagery	*Paradox*	*Attitude*
Metaphor	*Conflict (all kinds)*	*Theme*
Parallelism	*Foreshadowing*	*Satire*
Personification	*Rising action*	*Symbol*
Simile	*Denouement*	*Point of view*
Voice	*Narration*	

These make his narrative come alive and give it poetical quality. They make the reading of it very enjoyable.

_____
_____
_____
_____
_____
_____
_____
_____
_____
_____

Frederick Douglass

Narrative of the Life of Frederick Douglass (Chapter X-Appendix)

Week 34

Writing Assignment:

This week you will write your final essay for the year.
Review the guidelines in *Write With The Best, Vol. 2* for writing an expository essay (pages 94-95). This essay will be more expository because your facts will come from the texts you are comparing. Remember to use enough examples in your essay and to list the similarities and differences between the two works.
Use the proofreading checklist at the back of *Write With the Best, Vol. 2* to proofread and grade your essay.

FREDERICK DOUGLASS
NARRATIVE OF THE LIFE OF FREDERICK DOUGLASS (CHAPTER X- APPENDIX)

WEEK 34

CULMINATING ACTIVITY:

Alone or in a group, cast your vote for each of the following from the literary works you have read this year:

1) Work with most descriptive writing _____

2) Author who wrote with most suspense _____

3) Most entertaining author _____

4) Most inspiring work you read _____

5) Most memorable work (the one you can't forget) _____

6) Best poem _____

7) Saddest or most dismal author _____

8) Least favorite author _____

9) Favorite work overall _____

10) Favorite author overall _____

Read With The Best
— American Literature Volume I
Vocab Test

Vocabulary Test Weeks 1-4

Match the number of the word next to the letter of its meaning.

1. unfurled	13. feigned
2. infirm	14. insolent
3. superfluity	15. sloth
4. untoward	16. propensity
5. derision	17. requital
6. mollified	18. maxim
7. magnanimity	19. irrevocable
8. posterity	20. bereft
9. dissolute	21. visage
10. profane	22. felicity
11. solace	23. verity
12. quelled	

____A. laziness, idleness, inactivity

____B. ability, aptness

____C. lacking, missing, deprived

____D. offspring, descendant

____E. blasphemous, unholy, unsacred

____F. appearance, face, expression

____G. abundance, excess

____H. happiness, contentment

____I. corrupt, debase

____J. soothed, softened, pacified

____K. faked, pretended, acted

____L. generosity, philanthropy

____M. unchanged, fixed, certain

____N. unfolded

____O. payment, retaliation

____P. weak, faint, sick

____Q. conquered, crushed, suppressed

____R. ridicule, scorn

____S. a saying, adage, proverb

____T. truth, accuracy

____U. rude, disrespectful

____V. disobedient, defiant, unruly

____W. comfort, relief

Copyright © 2012 by Jill J. Dixon and T.L. Dixon www.edudps.com

Read With The Best
- American Literature Volume I

Vocab Test

Vocabulary Test Weeks 1-4

Match the number of the word next to the letter of its meaning.

1. unfurled	13. feigned
2. infirm	14. insolent
3. superfluity	15. sloth
4. untoward	16. propensity
5. derision	17. requital
6. mollified	18. maxim
7. magnanimity	19. irrevocable
8. posterity	20. bereft
9. dissolute	21. visage
10. profane	22. felicity
11. solace	23. verity
12. quelled	

_15_ A. laziness, idleness, inactivity

_16_ B. ability, aptness

_20_ C. lacking, missing, deprived

_8_ D. offspring, descendant

_10_ E. blasphemous, unholy, unsacred

_21_ F. appearance, face, expression

_3_ G. abundance, excess

_22_ H. happiness, contentment

_9_ I. corrupt, debase

_6_ J. soothed, softened, pacified

_13_ K. faked, pretended, acted

_7_ L. generosity, philanthropy

_19_ M. unchanged, fixed, certain

_1_ N. unfolded

_17_ O. payment, retaliation

_2_ P. weak, faint, sick

_12_ Q. conquered, crushed, suppressed

_5_ R. ridicule, scorn

_18_ S. a saying, adage, proverb

_23_ T. truth, accuracy

_14_ U. rude, disrespectful

_4_ V. disobedient, defiant, unruly

_11_ W. comfort, relief

Copyright © 2012 by Jill J. Dixon and T.L. Dixon

www.edudps.com

Read With The Best
- American Literature Volume I

Vocab Test

Vocabulary Test Weeks 5-8

Match the number of the word next to the letter of its meaning.

1. din	15. conundrum
2. disconsolate	16. contrivance
3. doleful	17. potent
4. infidel	18. dolorous
5. lamentable	19. mitigation
6. melancholy	20. affable
7. abate	21. fractious
8. extirpation	22. inducements
9. halcyon	23. apparitor
10. malefactor	24. dissuade
11. sundry	25. diffidence
12. prodigious	26. eminent
13. deposed	27. errata
14. parsimony	

___A. assorted, various

___B. famous, celebrated, very important

___C. removed from a high position, demoted

___D. depression, sadness, dejection

___E. calm, harmonious, gentle

___F. loud, continuous noise

___G. plan, design, fabrication

___H. destruction, annihilation, extermination

___I. huge, large, amazing

___J. unbeliever, heretic

___K. afflicted, miserable, anguished, dire

___L. lessen, diminish, decrease

___M. unable to be consoled, unhappy

___N. bad criminal, sinner, evil person

___O. powerful, forceful, effective

___P. alleviation, reduction, cure, relief

___Q. motives, causes, incentives

___R. upsetting, awful, to be mourned

___S. stinginess, frugality, miserliness

___T. talk out of, advise or caution against

___U. doubt, fear, hesitancy

___V. error, mistake, misprint

___W. friendly, benevolent, cordial, amiable

___X. an officer or civil servant

___Y. problem, puzzle, mystery

___Z. grouchy, cross, contentious

Copyright © 2012 by Jill J. Dixon and T.L. Dixon   www.edudps.com

Read With The Best
- American Literature Volume I

Vocab Test

Vocabulary Test Weeks 5-8

Match the number of the word next to the letter of its meaning.

1. din	15. conundrum
2. disconsolate	16. contrivance
3. doleful	17. potent
4. infidel	18. dolorous
5. lamentable	19. mitigation
6. melancholy	20. affable
7. abate	21. fractious
8. extirpation	22. inducements
9. halcyon	23. apparitor
10. malefactor	24. dissuade
11. sundry	25. diffidence
12. prodigious	26. eminent
13. deposed	27. errata
14. parsimony	

_11_ A. assorted, various

_26_ B. famous, celebrated, very important

_13_ C. removed from a high position, demoted

_6_ D. depression, sadness, dejection

_9_ E. calm, harmonious, gentle

_1_ F. loud, continuous noise

_16_ G. plan, design, fabrication

_8_ H. destruction, annihilation, extermination

_12_ I. huge, large, amazing

_4_ J. unbeliever, heretic

_18_ K. afflicted, miserable, anguished, dire

_7_ L. lessen, diminish, decrease

_2_ M. unable to be consoled, unhappy

_10_ N. bad criminal, sinner, evil person

_17_ O. powerful, forceful, effective

_19_ P. alleviation, reduction, cure, relief

_22_ Q. motives, causes, incentives

_5_ R. upsetting, awful, to be mourned

_14_ S. stinginess, frugality, miserliness

_24_ T. talk out of, advise or caution against

_25_ U. doubt, fear, hesitancy

_27_ V. error, mistake, misprint

_20_ W. friendly, benevolent, cordial, amiable

_23_ X. an officer or civil servant

_15_ Y. problem, puzzle, mystery

_21_ Z. grouchy, cross, contentious

Read With The Best
- American Literature Volume I

Vocab Test

Vocabulary Test Weeks 9-12

Match the number of the word next to the letter of its meaning.

1. remit
2. ingenious
3. conferred
4. facetious
5. genteel
6. jocular
7. sagacious
8. traduce
9. arduous
10. sanguine
11. augmented
12. avarice
13. insolent
14. harangue
15. solicitous
16. irresolute
17. dissipate
18. pernicious
19. languid
20. relinquish
21. fallacious
22. sycophant
23. complicit

____A. amusing, comical, sarcastic, witty

____B. puppet, slave, person who caters to another

____C. difficult, burdensome, harsh, hard

____D. cultured, sophisticated, aristocratic

____E. worried, anxious, apprehensive, very careful

____F. guilty in a crime or an offense

____G. dull, comatose, listless, weak, sluggish, slow

____H. send, transfer, dispatch

____I. smart, judicious, acute (sharp)

____J. extreme greed, frugality

____K. to slander, disagree, violate

____L. long lecture, speech, address

____M. clever, brilliant, intelligent

____N. happy, cheerful, optimistic

____O. doubtful, changing, indecisive

____P. made greater, improved

____Q. funny, playful, cheerful, jolly, jesting

____R. disrespectful, bold, arrogant

____S. discussed, consulted, advised

____T. spend, consume

____U. bad, dangerous, hurtful

____V. give up, let go, abandon

____W. false, incorrect, deceptive

Copyright © 2012 by Jill J. Dixon and T.L. Dixon

www.edudps.com

Read With The Best
- American Literature Volume I

Vocab Test

Vocabulary Test Weeks 9-12

Match the number of the word next to the letter of its meaning.

1. remit	13. insolent
2. ingenious	14. harangue
3. conferred	15. solicitous
4. facetious	16. irresolute
5. genteel	17. dissipate
6. jocular	18. pernicious
7. sagacious	19. languid
8. traduce	20. relinquish
9. arduous	21. fallacious
10. sanguine	22. sycophant
11. augmented	23. complicit
12. avarice	

_4_ A. amusing, comical, sarcastic, witty

_22_ B. puppet, slave, person who caters to another

_9_ C. difficult, burdensome, harsh, hard

_5_ D. cultured, sophisticated, aristocratic

_15_ E. worried, anxious, apprehensive, very careful

_23_ F. guilty in a crime or an offense

_19_ G. dull, comatose, listless, weak, sluggish, slow

_1_ H. send, transfer, dispatch

_7_ I. smart, judicious, acute (sharp)

_12_ J. extreme greed, frugality

_8_ K. to slander, disagree, violate

_14_ L. long lecture, speech, address

_2_ M. clever, brilliant, intelligent

_10_ N. happy, cheerful, optimistic

_16_ O. doubtful, changing, indecisive

_11_ P. made greater, improved

_6_ Q. funny, playful, cheerful, jolly, jesting

_13_ R. disrespectful, bold, arrogant

_3_ S. discussed, consulted, advised

_17_ T. disperse, spend, throw away, waste

_18_ U. bad, dangerous, hurtful

_20_ V. give up, let go, abandon

_21_ W. false, incorrect, deceptive

Copyright © 2012 by Jill J. Dixon and T.L. Dixon

www.edudps.com

Read With The Best
- American Literature Volume I

Vocab Test

Vocabulary Test Weeks 13-16

Match the number of the word next to the letter of its meaning.

1. avert	13. alacrity
2. insidious	14. malleable
3. complaisance	15. insuperable
4. pusillanimous	16. uncouth
5. diabolic	17. disputatious
6. propitious	18. impunity
7. pensive	19. venerable
8. scrupulous	20. discordant
9. obsequious	21. indurated
10. decried	22. guile
11. conciliating	23. illimitable
12. wistfully	

____A. full of promise, favorable, hopeful, encouraging

____B. longingly, sadly, daydreaming(ly)

____C. respected, admirable, aged

____D. evil, demonic, cruel

____E. submissive, excessively humble or obedient

____F. liveliness, eagerness, enthusiasm, cheerful readiness

____G. avoid, turn away, thwart

____H. appeasing, pacifying, alleviating

____I. not in harmony, antagonistic, conflicting

____J. extremely careful, conscientious, exact

____K. deceit, cunning

____L. sneaky, tricky, crafty

____M. cowardly, timid, helpless

____N. discovered, detected

____O. argumentative, contentious

____P. endless, constant, everlasting

____Q. pliable, adaptable

____R. contemplative, meditative, solemn

____S. freedom, liberty, exemption

____T. disposition to please

____U. coarse, uncultivated, clumsy, barbaric

____V. impossible, overwhelming, insurmountable

____W. hardened, calloused, physically or emotionally hardened

Bonus: Pick 3 words and write a sentence to describe an author or work we have read this year.

Read With The Best
- American Literature Volume I

Vocab Test

Vocabulary Test Weeks 13-16

Match the number of the word next to the letter of its meaning.

1. avert	13. alacrity
2. insidious	14. malleable
3. complaisance	15. insuperable
4. pusillanimous	16. uncouth
5. diabolic	17. disputatious
6. propitious	18. impunity
7. pensive	19. venerable
8. scrupulous	20. discordant
9. obsequious	21. indurated
10. decried	22. guile
11. conciliating	23. illimitable
12. wistfully	

__6__ A. full of promise, favorable, hopeful, encouraging

__12__ B. longingly, sadly, daydreaming(ly)

__19__ C. respected, admirable, aged

__5__ D. evil, demonic, cruel

__9__ E. submissive, excessively humble or obedient

__13__ F. liveliness, eagerness, enthusiasm, cheerful readiness

__1__ G. avoid, turn away, thwart

__11__ H. appeasing, pacifying, alleviating

__20__ I. not in harmony, antagonistic, conflicting

__8__ J. extremely careful, conscientious, exact

__22__ K. deceit, cunning

__2__ L. sneaky, tricky, crafty

__4__ M. cowardly, timid, helpless

__10__ N. discovered, detected

__17__ O. argumentative, contentious

__23__ P. endless, constant, everlasting

__14__ Q. pliable, adaptable

__7__ R. contemplative, meditative, solemn

__18__ S. freedom, liberty, exemption

__3__ T. disposition to please

__16__ U. coarse, uncultivated, clumsy, barbaric

__15__ V. impossible, overwhelming, insurmountable

__21__ W. hardened, calloused, physically or emotionally hardened

Bonus: Pick 3 words and write a sentence to describe an author or work we have read this year. Answers will vary.

Copyright © 2012 by Jill J. Dixon and T.L. Dixon   www.edudps.com

Read With The Best
- American Literature Volume I

Vocab Test

Vocabulary Test Weeks 17-20

Match the number of the word next to the letter of its meaning.

1. anomaly	14. indubitably
2. fetish	15. ignominy
3. nebulous	16. congenial
4. pecuniary	17. mien
5. undulation	18. sagacity
6. auspicious	19. expostulation
7. tempestuous	20. prolific
8. ocular	21. insidious
9. similitude	22. caprice
10. anathema	23. imperious
11. abash	24. antiquated
12. antipathy	25. bibliomaniac
13. expedient	26. ostentatious

____A. financial, relating to money

____B. agreeable, nice, harmonious

____C. violent, explosive, stormy

____D. wisdom, discernment, perception

____E. a wavy motion or pulsation of sound

____F. undeniable, unquestionable

____G. an object, challenge or complaint

____H. abnormality, something irregular or unnatural

____I. productive, fruitful, rich

____J. similarity, resemblance, likeness

____K. indefinite, vague, unclear

____L. demeanor, mood, appearance

____M. encouraging, promising success, prosperous

____N. a whim, sudden inclination to do things impulsively

____O. obsession, fixation or charm

____P. domineering, commanding, compelling

____Q. beneficial, profitable, advantageous

____R. outdated, obsolete, outmoded

____S. a person or thing accursed, curse, abomination

____T. a lover of books

____U. dishonor, disgrace, shame

____V. loud, flashy, pompous

____W. embarrass, confuse, rattle

____X. animosity, bitterness, hostility, dislike

____Y. sly, subtle, treacherous, seductive

____Z. visual, relating to the eye

Bonus: Use 3 of the words to describe an author or work from this year.

Read With The Best
- American Literature Volume I

Vocab Test

Vocabulary Test Weeks 17-20

Match the number of the word next to the letter of its meaning.

1. anomaly	14. indubitably
2. fetish	15. ignominy
3. nebulous	16. congenial
4. pecuniary	17. mien
5. undulation	18. sagacity
6. auspicious	19. expostulation
7. tempestuous	20. prolific
8. ocular	21. insidious
9. similitude	22. caprice
10. anathema	23. imperious
11. abash	24. antiquated
12. antipathy	25. bibliomaniac
13. expedient	26. ostentatious

__4__ A. financial, relating to money

__16__ B. agreeable, nice, harmonious

__7__ C. violent, explosive, stormy

__18__ D. wisdom, discernment, perception

__5__ E. a wavy motion or pulsation of sound

__14__ F. undeniable, unquestionable

__19__ G. an object, challenge or complaint

__1__ H. abnormality, something irregular or unnatural

__20__ I. productive, fruitful, rich

__9__ J. similarity, resemblance, likeness

__3__ K. indefinite, vague, unclear

__17__ L. demeanor, mood, appearance

__6__ M. encouraging, promising success, prosperous

__22__ N. a whim, sudden inclination to do things impulsively

__2__ O. obsession, fixation or charm

__23__ P. domineering, commanding, compelling

__13__ Q. beneficial, profitable, advantageous

__24__ R. outdated, obsolete, outmoded

__10__ S. a person or thing accursed, curse, abomination

__25__ T. a lover of books

__15__ U. dishonor, disgrace, shame

__26__ V. loud, flashy, pompous

__11__ W. embarrass, confuse, rattle

__12__ X. animosity, bitterness, hostility, dislike

__21__ Y. sly, subtle, treacherous, seductive

__8__ Z. visual, relating to the eye

Bonus: *Use 3 of the words to describe an author or work from this year.*

Answers will vary.

Read With The Best
- American Literature Volume I

Vocab Test

Vocabulary Test Weeks 21-24

Match the number of the word next to the letter of its meaning.

1. infamy	13. obviate
2. importunate	14. sedulous
3. efficacy	15. asperity
4. affinity	16. misanthropy
5. inimical	17. duplicity
6. wary	18. pithy
7. latent	19. inducement
8. odious	20. languidly
9. scurrilous	21. surmise
10. abase	22. lurid
11. repose	23. disquietude
12. despotic	24. scintillate

___A. deceit, dishonesty, double-dealing

___B. weakly, sluggishly, faintly, softly, slowly

___C. to lay at rest, to lie dead, sleep, calm, peace

___D. prevent, avert, forestall

___E. guess, assume, speculate, suspect

___F. attraction toward, sympathy toward, relationship to

___G. something that convinces or persuades, a motive, convincing persuasion

___H. to flash, glimmer, glitter, sparkle, gleam

___I. inactive, not visible, dead, dormant

___J. obscene, vulgar, coarsely joking

___K. ghostly pale in appearance, pale, gruesome

___L. an evil reputation, fame for evil or criminal reasons

___M. to lower in rank or esteem, to humble or degrade

___N. busy, active, diligent, working, engaged

___O. very cautious, careful, alert

___P. having substance, concise, brief

___Q. troublesomely urgent or persistent, burdensome

___R. roughness, harshness, difficulty, hardship

___S. overbearing, bossy, tyrannical

___T. efficiency, capability, ability, productiveness

___U. anxiety, agitation, uneasiness, worry

___V. hatred of mankind

___W. hostile, unfriendly, having the disposition of an enemy

___X. deserving or causing hatred, appalling, abominable, offensive

Bonus: *Write one sentence with 3 of the words. Use the words correctly.*

Read With The Best
- American Literature Volume I

Vocab Test

Vocabulary Test Weeks 21-24

Match the number of the word next to the letter of its meaning.

1. infamy	13. obviate
2. importunate	14. sedulous
3. efficacy	15. asperity
4. affinity	16. misanthropy
5. inimical	17. duplicity
6. wary	18. pithy
7. latent	19. inducement
8. odious	20. languidly
9. scurrilous	21. surmise
10. abase	22. lurid
11. repose	23. disquietude
12. despotic	24. scintillate

__17__ A. deceit, dishonesty, double-dealing

__20__ B. weakly, sluggishly, faintly, softly, slowly

__11__ C. to lay at rest, to lie dead, sleep, calm, peace

__13__ D. prevent, avert, forestall

__21__ E. guess, assume, speculate, suspect

__4__ F. attraction toward, sympathy toward, relationship to

__19__ G. something that convinces or persuades, a motive, convincing persuasion

__24__ H. to flash, glimmer, glitter, sparkle, gleam

__7__ I. inactive, not visible, dead, dormant

__9__ J. obscene, vulgar, coarsely joking

__22__ K. ghostly pale in appearance, pale, gruesome

__1__ L. an evil reputation, fame for evil or criminal reasons

__10__ M. to lower in rank or esteem, to humble or degrade

__14__ N. busy, active, diligent, working, engaged

__6__ O. very cautious, careful, alert

__18__ P. having substance, concise, brief

__2__ Q. troublesomely urgent or persistent, burdensome

__15__ R. roughness, harshness, difficulty, hardship

__12__ S. overbearing, bossy, tyrannical

__3__ T. efficiency, capability, ability, productiveness

__23__ U. anxiety, agitation, uneasiness, worry

__16__ V. hatred of mankind

__5__ W. hostile, unfriendly, having the disposition of an enemy

__8__ X. deserving or causing hatred, appalling, abominable, offensive

**Bonus: Write one sentence with 3 of the words. Use the words correctly.
Answers will vary.**

Copyright © 2012 by Jill J. Dixon and T.L. Dixon

www.edudps.com

Read With The Best
- American Literature Volume I

Vocab Test

Vocabulary Test Weeks 25-34

Match the number of the word next to the letter of its meaning.

1. surcease	13. inebriate
2. obeisance	14. civility
3. dissever	15. inexpedient
4. affinity	16. requisitions
5. distempered	17. gregariousness
6. interment	18. profligate
7. munificent	19. obdurate
8. remunerate	20. requiem
9. abrogation	21. factitious
10. recondite	22. palatable
11. imperative	23. imprudent
12. execrable; execrate	24. interposed

___A. confused, disturbed

___B. horrific, detestable -
    to condemn or despise

___C. an ending or discontinuation

___D. unwise, futile

___E. giving or generous

___F. pleasant, agreeable, satisfying

___G. a degenerate or prodigal

___H. to make drunk or intoxicate

___I. a hymn or song
    for a person who has died

___J. important, necessary

___K. a fondness or attraction

___L. friendship, sociability

___M. to stop, delay, resist

___N. indiscreet, unwise

___O. mysterious or mystical

___P. appeals, demands

___Q. courtesy or graciousness

___R. reverence or allegiance

___S. fake, false, artificial

___T. obstinate, hardheaded

___U. burial

___V. intruded, interrupted, placed between

___W. to reward, pay, or award

___X to separate or cut off

Bonus: Write one sentence with 3 of the words. Use the words correctly.

_____
_____
_____
_____

Read With The Best
- American Literature Volume I

Vocab Test

Vocabulary Test Weeks 25-34

Match the number of the word next to the letter of its meaning.

1. surcease	13. inebriate
2. obeisance	14. civility
3. dissever	15. inexpedient
4. affinity	16. requisitions
5. distempered	17. gregariousness
6. interment	18. profligate
7. munificent	19. obdurate
8. remunerate	20. requiem
9. abrogation	21. factitious
10. recondite	22. palatable
11. imperative	23. imprudent
12. execrable; execrate	24. interposed

__5__ A. confused, disturbed

__12__ B. horrific, detestable – to condemn or despise

__9__ C. an ending or discontinuation

__15__ D. unwise, futile

__7__ E. giving or generous

__22__ F. pleasant, agreeable, satisfying

__18__ G. a degenerate or prodigal

__13__ H. to make drunk or intoxicate

__20__ I. a hymn or song for a person who has died

__11__ J. important, necessary

__4__ K. a fondness or attraction

__17__ L. friendship, sociability

__1__ M. to stop, delay, resist

__23__ N. indiscreet, unwise

__10__ O. mysterious or mystical

__16__ P. appeals, demands

__14__ Q. courtesy or graciousness

__2__ R. reverence or allegiance

__21__ S. fake, false, artificial

__19__ T. obstinate, hardheaded

__6__ U. burial

__24__ V. intruded, interrupted, placed between

__8__ W. to reward, pay, or award

__3__ X. to separate or cut off

Bonus: Write one sentence with 3 of the words. Use the words correctly.

Answers will vary.

Read With The Best
- American Literature Volume I

Lit. Terms Test

Literary Terms Test Weeks 1-6

Match the number of the word next to the letter of its meaning.

1. synecdoche	10. allusion
2. personification	11. metaphor
3. narration	12. tone
4. point of view	13. iambic couplet
5. omniscient point of view	14. conceit
6. limited omniscient point of view	15. simile
7. objective point of view	16. genre
8. stream of consciousness	17. anaphora
9. parallelism or parallel structure	

____A. A comparison of 2 things without the use of "like" or "as."

____B. The narrator only reports what a camera can see or what someone would hear the character speak.

____C. The perspective from which a literary work is presented; there are 3 main types.

____D. A brief reference to a famous person, event or condition.

____E. First person point of view revealing the inward thoughts of the main character usually as illogical or haphazard.

____F. A figure of speech that gives nonhuman objects or abstract ideas human qualities or features.

____G. A narrator, like God, sees into each character's mind and knows everything that goes on.

____H. A comparison (or metaphor) of 2 unlikely things that is drawn out within a poem.

____I. The repetition of the same words at the beginning of successive phrases.

____J. A type of writing that tells a story.

____K. The use of the same forms of verbs and sometimes nouns or phrases to show emphasis or draw attention in writing.

____L. Two successive lines of rhyming poetry that have a rhythmic pattern of an unaccented syllable followed by an accented syllable.

____M. A comparison of 2 things using "like" or "as."

____N. The narrator only has knowledge of one character (usually the main character).

____O. A figure of speech in which a part of something stands for the whole.

____P. The kind or type of a work of literature.

____Q. The author's attitude toward his subject.

Bonus: Write your own example of two of these terms.

Copyright © 2012 by Jill J. Dixon and T.L. Dixon   www.edudps.com

Read With The Best
- American Literature Volume I

Lit. Terms Test

Literary Terms Test Weeks 1-6

Match the number of the word next to the letter of its meaning.

1. synecdoche	10. allusion
2. personification	11. metaphor
3. narration	12. tone
4. point of view	13. iambic couplet
5. omniscient point of view	14. conceit
6. limited omniscient point of view	15. simile
7. objective point of view	16. genre
8. stream of consciousness	17. anaphora
9. parallelism or parallel structure	

_11_ A. A comparison of 2 things without the use of "like" or "as."

_7_ B. The narrator only reports what a camera can see or what someone would hear the character speak.

_4_ C. The perspective from which a literary work is presented; there are 3 main types.

_10_ D. A brief reference to a famous person, event or condition.

_8_ E. First person point of view revealing the inward thoughts of the main character usually as illogical or haphazard.

_2_ F. A figure of speech that gives nonhuman objects or abstract ideas human qualities or features.

_5_ G. A narrator, like God, sees into each character's mind and knows everything that goes on.

_14_ H. A comparison (or metaphor) of 2 unlikely things that is drawn out within a poem.

_17_ I. The repetition of the same words at the beginning of successive phrases.

_3_ J. A type of writing that tells a story.

_9_ K. The use of the same forms of verbs and sometimes nouns or phrases to show emphasis or draw attention in writing.

_13_ L. Two successive lines of rhyming poetry that have a rhythmic pattern of an unaccented syllable followed by an accented syllable.

_15_ M. A comparison of 2 things using "like" or "as."

_6_ N. The narrator only has knowledge of one character (usually the main character).

_1_ O. A figure of speech in which a part of something stands for the whole.

_16_ P. The kind or type of a work of literature.

_12_ Q. The author's attitude toward his subject.

Bonus: Write your own example of two of these terms. *Answers will vary.*

Copyright © 2012 by Jill J. Dixon and T.L. Dixon   www.edudps.com

Read With The Best
- American Literature Volume I

Lit. Terms Test

Literary Terms Test Weeks 7-12

Match the number of the word next to the letter of its meaning.

1. imagery	6. style
2. metaphysical conceit	7. aphorism
3. diction	8. voice
4. periodic sentence	9. alliteration
5. syntax	

_____ A. A brief saying intended to teach a truth or belief.

_____ B. The speaker's or narrator's view on a specific idea expressed in a literary passage.

_____ C. The repetition of usually initial consonant sounds.

_____ D. The way words or clauses are arranged in a sentence.

_____ E. An extended metaphor that uses lofty and elaborate language and imaginative images and intense emotion.

_____ F. The choice and use of words and the emphasis with which they are spoken.

_____ G. The main clause or full meaning is not given until the end.

_____ H. Any sensory detail the author uses to paint word pictures in the mind of the reader.

_____ I. The unique way a writer arranges words and expresses himself and can include diction, syntax, and figurative language.

J. Give an example of alliteration.

Bonus: Give an example of a periodic sentence or an aphorism.

Copyright © 2012 by Jill J. Dixon and T.L. Dixon   www.edudps.com

Read With The Best
– American Literature Volume I

Lit. Terms Test

Literary Terms Test Weeks 7-12

Match the number of the word next to the letter of its meaning.

1. imagery (47)	6. style
2. metaphysical conceit (47)	7. aphorism
3. diction (56)	8. voice (75)
4. periodic sentence (63)	9. alliteration (82)
5. syntax (63)	

__7__ A. A brief saying intended to teach a truth or belief.

__8__ B. The speaker's or narrator's view on a specific idea expressed in a literary passage.

__9__ C. The repetition of usually initial consonant sounds.

__5__ D. The way words or clauses are arranged in a sentence.

__2__ E. An extended metaphor that uses lofty and elaborate language and imaginative images and intense emotion.

__3__ F. The choice and use of words and the emphasis with which they are spoken.

__4__ G. The main clause or full meaning is not given until the end.

__1__ H. Any sensory detail the author uses to paint word pictures in the mind of the reader.

__6__ I. The unique way a writer arranges words and expresses himself and can include diction, syntax, and figurative language.

J. Give an example of alliteration. **Answers will vary.**

Bonus: Give an example of a periodic sentence or an aphorism. Answers will vary.

theme (p97)
symbol (p97)
Transcendentalism (p104)
Amer. Renaissance (p120)
Internal Rhyme (p120)
Free Verse (p120)
Antithesis (p208)

Copyright © 2012 by Jill J. Dixon and T.L. Dixon　　　www.edudps.com

Read With The Best
– American Literature Volume I

Lit. Terms Test

Literary Terms Test Weeks 13-18

Match the number of the word next to the letter of its meaning.

1. rhetoric	10. apostrophe
2. rhetorical question	11. blank verse
3. theme	12. elegy
4. symbol	13. American Renaissance
5. satire	14. internal rhyme
6. stereotype or stock character	15. free verse
7. round character	16. prose
8. Romanticism	17. allegory
9. Transcendentalism	18. parable

___A. Poetry that lacks regular meter, rhythm, and rhyme length.
___B. The art of using words to persuade.
___C. A figure of speech in which the speaker talks directly to something nonhuman or someone not present.
___D. A character who appears so often in writing that he is immediately recognizable.
___E. The ordinary form of written language without metircal or rhythmic form.
___F. Poetry written in unrhymed iambic pentameter. It does not rhyme but does have a regular rhythm.
___G. The central and dominating idea in a literary work.
___H. A short, simple story that teaches a lesson.
___I. Emphasized imagination and emotion over reason, the supernatural over common sense, and the supremacy of the individual over tradition.
___J. A story in which characters, actions or settings represent ideas or qualities.
___K. Used in persuasive writing to produce an effect or make a statement, but is not expected to be answered.
___L. An object, image, feeling, or color that represents or stands for something else.
___M. Time period in which some of America's most influential writers wrote.
___N. Rhyme occurring at the middle and end of a metrical line of poetry.
___O. A literary technique that blends humor with the ridiculing of thoughts and weaknesses of mankind.
___P. A type of poem that meditates on death or mortality.
___Q. Emphasized the importance of the individual conscience and intuition and believed God's moral law is revealed in nature.
___R. The character who is fully developed, complex, and stands out from the other characters as an individual.

BONUS: Give an example of 3 of the literary terms for 5 extra points.

Copyright © 2012 by Jill J. Dixon and T.L. Dixon www.edudps.com

READ WITH THE BEST
- AMERICAN LITERATURE VOLUME I

LIT. TERMS TEST

LITERARY TERMS TEST WEEKS 13-18

Match the number of the word next to the letter of its meaning.

1. rhetoric	10. apostrophe
2. rhetorical question	11. blank verse
3. theme	12. elegy
4. symbol	13. American Renaissance
5. satire	14. internal rhyme
6. stereotype or stock character	15. free verse
7. round character	16. prose
8. Romanticism	17. allegory
9. Transcendentalism	18. parable

__15__ A. Poetry that lacks regular meter, rhythm, and rhyme length.
__1__ B. The art of using words to persuade.
__10__ C. A figure of speech in which the speaker talks directly to something nonhuman or someone not present.
__6__ D. A character who appears so often in writing that he is immediately recognizable.
__16__ E. The ordinary form of written language without metircal or rhythmic form.
__11__ F. Poetry written in unrhymed iambic pentameter. It does not rhyme but does have a regular rhythm.
__3__ G. The central and dominating idea in a literary work.
__18__ H. A short, simple story that teaches a lesson.
__8__ I. Emphasized imagination and emotion over reason, the supernatural over common sense, and the supremacy of the individual over tradition.
__17__ J. A story in which characters, actions or settings represent ideas or qualities.
__2__ K. Used in persuasive writing to produce an object or make a statement, but is not expected to be answered.
__4__ L. An object, image, feeling, or color that represents or stands for something else.
__13__ M. Time period in which some of America's most influential writers wrote.
__14__ N. Rhyme occurring at the middle and end of a metrical line of poetry.
__5__ O. A literary technique that blends humor with the ridiculing of thoughts and weaknesses of mankind.
__12__ P. A type of poem that meditates on death or mortality.
__9__ Q. Emphasized the importance of the individual conscience and intuition and believed God's moral law is revealed in nature.
__7__ R. The character who is fully developed, complex, and stands out from the other characters as an individual.

Bonus: Give an example of 3 of the literary terms for 5 extra points. *Answers will vary.*

Read With The Best
- American Literature Volume I

Lit. Terms Test

Literary Terms Test Weeks 19-24

Match the number of the word next to the letter of its meaning.

1. situational irony	8. social conflict
2. dramatic irony	9. internal/psychological conflict
3. paradox	10. foreshadowing
4. crisis	11. rising action
5. climax	12. didactic/didacticism
6. conflict	13. denouement/resolution/falling action
7. physical conflict	

___A. Extreme conflict of a plot in a literary work which leads to the climax.

___B. The struggle between man and man, man and society or man and fate.

___C. When facts or situations that are different from what is expected are known to readers or the audience, but not the character.

___D. The part of a plot that involves complication and conflict and leads up to the climax.

___E. The turning point in a literary work where the crisis comes to its point of greatest intensity and is resolved to some degree.

___F. The opposition of persons or forces upon which the action and plot depend.

___G. The use of writing for teaching and offering moral, religious or ethical guidance.

___H. A showing, indication, or suggestion of what will happen later in a literary work.

___I. The final outcome of the plot where everything is resolved. This comes after the climax.

___J. The struggle between man and the physical world such as nature.

___K. The struggle between desires within a person.

___L. When events or situations in a literary work end up the opposite of what is expected.

___M. A self-contradictory or absurd statement that is actually true.

BONUS: From the list of literary terms, give 2 examples from literature we have read this year.

READ WITH THE BEST
– *American Literature Volume I*

LIT. TERMS TEST

LITERARY TERMS TEST WEEKS 19-24

Match the number of the word next to the letter of its meaning.

1. situational irony	8. social conflict
2. dramatic irony	9. internal/psychological conflict
3. paradox	10. foreshadowing
4. crisis	11. rising action
5. climax	12. didactic/didacticism
6. conflict	13. denouement/resolution/falling action
7. physical conflict	

__4__ A. Extreme conflict of a plot in a literary work which leads to the climax.

__8__ B. The struggle between man and man, man and society or man and fate.

__2__ C. When facts or situations that are different from what is expected are known to readers or the audience, but not the character.

__11__ D. The part of a plot that involves complication and conflict and leads up to the climax.

__5__ E. The turning point in a literary work where the crisis comes to its point of greatest intensity and is resolved to some degree.

__6__ F. The opposition of persons or forces upon which the action and plot depend.

__12__ G. The use of writing for teaching and offering moral, religious or ethical guidance.

__10__ H. A showing, indication, or suggestion of what will happen later in a literary work.

__13__ I. The final outcome of the plot where everything is resolved. This comes after the climax.

__7__ J. The struggle between man and the physical world such as nature.

__9__ K. The struggle between desires within a person.

__1__ L. When events or situations in a literary work end up the opposite of what is expected.

__3__ M. A self-contradictory or absurd statement that is actually true.

Bonus: From the list of literary terms, give 2 examples from literature we have read this year. Answers will vary.

READ WITH THE BEST
– American Literature Volume I

LIT. TERMS TEST

LITERARY TERMS TEST WEEKS 25-34

Match the number of the word next to the letter of its meaning.

1. denotation	11. consonance
2. connotation	12. antithesis
3. assonance	13. hyperbole
4. Gothic fiction	14. slant rhyme or approximate rhyme
5. detective story	15. enjambment
6. protagonist	16. chiasmus
7. foil	17. mood
8. antagonist	18. parody
9. quatrain	19. motif
10. ballad stanza	

___A. A genre in literature characterized by gloomy settings, violent action or terror, a mood of decay and the supernatural.
___B. The repetition of vowel sounds in poetry, usually in stressed syllables.
___C. The running of thought from one line, couplet, or stanza to the next.
___D. The leading and central character of a literary work.
___E. Four lines of poetry with a rhyme scheme of abcb often used in songs and nursery rhymes.
___F. The chief opponent of the main character of a literary work.
___G. An extreme exaggeration or overstatement used to make a point in literature.
___H. The most common English stanza form [or poem] consisting of four lines.
___I. The figurative or literary meaning of a word.
___J. A humorous and satirical writing that ridicules a person, event, situation, or serious work of literature.
___K. A figure of speech in which the order of the words in the first half of a parallel clause is reversed in the second half.
___L. The placement of sharply contrasting and contradictory ideas in parallel words, phrases, or ideas.
___M. Poe was recognized as the inventor of this.
___N. A repetition of consonant sounds especially at the end of words.
___O. A person or thing in a story that makes another person seem better or more prominent.
___P. The substitution of assonance [words with similar vowel sounds] for real rhyme.
___Q. The predominating atmosphere or tone of a literary work or the feeling that establishes this atmosphere.
___R. The dictionary and literal meaning of a word.
___S. A recurring feature such as a name, object, image or phrase in a work of literature that contributes to the theme in some way.

Bonus: Give an example of 2 of the above words – either make up an example or give one from the works we have read.

Copyright © 2012 by Jill J. Dixon and T.L. Dixon   www.edudps.com

Read With The Best
- American Literature Volume I

Lit. Terms Test

Literary Terms Test Weeks 25-34

Match the number of the word next to the letter of its meaning.

1. denotation	11. consonance
2. connotation	12. antithesis
3. assonance	13. hyperbole
4. Gothic fiction	14. slant rhyme or approximate rhyme
5. detective story	15. enjambment
6. protagonist	16. chiasmus
7. foil	17. mood
8. antagonist	18. parody
9. quatrain	19. motif
10. ballad stanza	

__4__ A. A genre in literature characterized by gloomy settings, violent action or terror, a mood of decay and the supernatural.
__3__ B. The repetition of vowel sounds in poetry, usually in stressed syllables.
__15__ C. The running of thought from one line, couplet, or stanza to the next.
__6__ D. The leading and central character of a literary work.
__10__ E. Four lines of poetry with a rhyme scheme of abcb often used in songs and nursery rhymes.
__8__ F. The chief opponent of the main character of a literary work.
__13__ G. An extreme exaggeration or overstatement used to make a point in literature.
__9__ H. The most common English stanza form [or poem] consisting of four lines.
__2__ I. The figurative or literary meaning of a word.
__18__ J. A humorous and satirical writing that ridicules a person, event, situation, or serious work of literature.
__16__ K. A figure of speech in which the order of the words in the first half of a parallel clause is reversed in the second half.
__12__ L. The placement of sharply contrasting and contradictory ideas in parallel words, phrases, or ideas.
__5__ M. Poe was recognized as the inventor of this.
__11__ N. A repetition of consonant sounds especially at the end of words.
__7__ O. A person or thing in a story that makes another person seem better or more prominent.
__14__ P. The substitution of assonance [words with similar vowel sounds] for real rhyme.
__17__ Q. The predominating atmosphere or tone of a literary work or the feeling that establishes this atmosphere.
__1__ R. The dictionary and literal meaning of a word.
__19__ S. A recurring feature such as a name, object, image or phrase in a work of literature that contributes to the theme in some way.

Bonus: Give an example of 2 of the above words – either make up an example or give one from the works we have read. *Answers will vary.*

Copyright © 2012 by Jill J. Dixon and T.L. Dixon   www.edudps.com

Research Paper | Guide

Research Paper Checklist
(Each item counts 10 point.)

- ☐ The subject pertains to our literary study and is narrowed into a manageable topic.

- ☐ There is a clear thesis statement in the first paragraph.

- ☐ There is an outline

- ☐ It is evident that adequate research has been done. (It is a <u>research</u> paper, not a report, and not an opinionated essay.)

- ☐ Works are cited correctly <u>within</u> the paper.

- ☐ There is no noticeable plagiarism. Everyone else's ideas have been cited or referenced.

- ☐ There is a "Works Cited" page done correctly.

- ☐ There is unity throughout - Every main idea of every paragraph relates to the thesis statement and there is a topic sentence for every paragraph.

- ☐ There are not many spelling or grammar errors - no more than 4 or 5. (The paper has been proofread adequately.)

- ☐ There is an adequate conclusion.

Visit us on the web at
www.edudps.com
for current special offerings and sales!

Language Arts – Writing, Vocabulary, Literature
Curricula and Career Guides
Special Needs Guides
Learning Styles Assessments and Guides
Diagnostic Assessments
and More!

Look for these additional titles:
***Read with the Best – Vol. II
American Literature 1860-1960
Read with the Best –
British Literature
Read with the Best –
World Literature***